Michael J. WALSH: THE HEART OF CHRIST IN THE
WRITINGS OF KARL RAHNER

Analecta Gregoriana

Cura Pontificiae Universitatis Gregorianae edita
Vol. 209. Series Facultatis Theologiae: sectio B, n. 67

MICHAEL J. WALSH

THE HEART OF CHRIST IN THE WRITINGS OF KARL RAHNER

An Investigation of
Its Christological Foundation as an Example
of the Relationship between Theology and Spirituality

UNIVERSITÀ GREGORIANA EDITRICE

ROMA 1977

MICHAEL J. WALSH

THE HEART OF CHRIST
IN THE WRITINGS OF KARL RAHNER

An Investigation of
Its Christological Foundation as an Example
of the Relationship between Theology and Spirituality

UNIVERSITÀ GREGORIANA EDITRICE
ROMA 1977

Quest'opera di Michael J. Walsh: THE HEART OF CHRIST IN THE WRITINGS OF KARL RAHNER è stata pubblicata con l'approvazione ecclesiastica dalla Università Gregoriana Editrice, Roma 1977, e stampata dalla Tipografia della Pontificia Università Gregoriana.

TABLE OF CONTENTS

CHAPTER I

THE HEART OF CHRIST IN THE WRITINGS OF KARL RAHNER

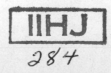

284

CHAPTER II

CHRISTOLOGICAL THEMES IN THE WRITINGS OF KARL RAHNER

CHAPTER III

THE VERIFICATION OF THE RAHNERIAN INTERPRETATION OF THE SYMBOL OF THE HEART OF CHRIST IN TERMS OF HIS CHRISTOLOGY

CHAPTER IV

CONCLUSION: SOME REFLECTIONS ON THE RELATIONSHIP BET-
WEEN THEOLOGY AND SPIRITUALITY AS THEY HAVE EMERGED
FROM THIS STUDY

DEDICATION

To my Mother,
To the memory of my Father:
Their love was my first intimation
Of the riches of the Love of Christ

The author gratefully acknowledges a grant from the International Institute of the Heart of Jesus which made the publication of this dissertation in the *Analecta Gregoriana* series possible.

ACKNOWLEDGEMENTS

A thesis represents one man's struggle to present his topic. Behind that struggle stands the help and support of many. The author wishes to acknowledge their contribution.

My thanks are due first of all to Most Rev. Francis J. Mugavero, D. D., Bishop of Brooklyn, for providing me with the opportunity to undertake graduate studies.

Rev. Robert Faricy, S.J., directed this thesis and deserves a word of thanks for his encouragement and helpful suggestions.

Rev. Karl Rahner, S.J., was very generous with his time in allowing me to interview him about the topic of this thesis.

Rev. Msgr. W. Stanley Fleming and the staff of the Casa Santa Maria dell'Umiltà deserve special thanks for providing a home away from home.

Revs. Michael Buckley, S.J., Edward Malatesta, S.J., William Murphy, Dennis Sheehan, John Vesey and Richard Ward have contributed, each in his own way, to the life of the author, and each knows why I thank him.

Sister Michacline O'Dwycr, R.S.H.M., was very generous with her time in typing the first draft of this thesis, and Harriet Rosenberg did an excellent job with the final copy.

Last, but not least, the loving support and prayers of many members of Holy Family Parish, Brooklyn, New York, deserve a special mention and the gratitude of their silent correspondent.

SIGLA

AAS	*Acta Apostolicae Sedis*
DS	Denzinger-Schönmetzer, *Enchiridion Symbolorum, Definitionum et Declarationum de Rebus Fidei et Morum*
I Th Q	*Irish Theological Quarterly*
K Th W	*Kleines Theologisches Wörterbuch*
NRT	*Nouvelle Revue Théologique*
RAM	*Revue d'Ascétique et Mystique*
RSPT	*Revue des Sciences Philosophiques et Théologiques*
Schriften	*Schriften zur Theologie*
T. I.	*Theological Investigations*
TDNT	*Theological Dictionary of the New Testament*
TS	*Theological Studies*

INTRODUCTION

Devotion to the Sacred Heart of Jesus was one of the most characteristic popular Catholic devotions of the Nineteenth and the first half of the Twentieth Centuries. Its living importance in Catholic life can be attested to by considering three facts: between 1899 and 1956, this Devotion was the subject of three papal encyclical letters; the *corpus* of theological literature on the subject of this Devotion is immense; most importantly, the Devotion was practiced with considerable enthusiasm by millions of Catholics throughout the world and provided a context for the regular reception of the sacraments in the pre-Vatican II era.

The years between 1945 and 1956 were a time of particularly lively theological discussion on the Devotion. This discussion grew out of the realization that the practice of the Devotion was no longer finding favor among the young. In an attempt to give new life to its practice, many theologians engaged themselves in the task of seeking to find new interpretations of and new insights about the Heart of Jesus. This era was marked in particular with a discussion of the object of the Devotion to the Heart of Christ and a discussion of the role of symbolism in the Devotion.

This thesis will concern itself with the contribution of Karl Rahner to that discussion. The theological system which Rahner has constructed for himself enabled him to make some original contributions to the discussion of the Sacred Heart Devotion. Rahner's contribution met with both enthusiastic approval and strong disagreement among his theological confreres.

The title of the thesis indicates the procedure we will follow in the presentation: "The Heart of Christ in the Writings of Karl Rahner: An Investigation of its Christological Foundation as an Example of the Relationship between Theology and Spirituality."

Chapter I comprises an analysis of Rahner's writings on the Sacred Heart. This analysis begins with the existential experience of symbols in human language. From this experience

Rahner develops an ontology of symbolism. This ontology is one of his major contributions to theology. Rahner developed this ontology specifically with the symbol of the Heart of Christ in mind. This ontology represents a clarification of the role of the symbol of the Heart of Christ in the Devotion. Rahner's theory of symbolism helps to unify the object of the Devotion while at the same time explaining the experience of symbolic activity in general. The presentation of Rahner's ontology of symbolism is followed by a presentation of his reflections on the Devotion itself. Because of the essential connection between the symbol and the person of Jesus, we see that the symbol of the Heart of Jesus, as Rahner understands it, communicates all the essential elements of a Christology. The first chapter concludes with a summary presentation of Rahner's critical reflections on the practices of the Devotion to the Sacred Heart.

Chapter II is essentially a middle step in the process of the thesis. Because of the Christological content of the symbol of the Heart as Rahner understands it, the second chapter is an attempt to present a general synthesis of the major themes of Rahner's Christology. In order to better understand Rahner's ideas on the symbol of the Sacred Heart, one must understand his Christological viewpoint. Specifically, Chapter II presents a synthesis of the "older" Rahner's Christology, i.e., the Christological viewpoint of Rahner at the time of his writings on the Sacred Heart. First we present Rahner's critique of traditional "school" Christology. Rahner formulates his critique on the basis of the dialectical formulation of the Council of Chalcedon. With this critique in mind, Rahner reflects on the mystery of Christ with the purpose of finding new formulations or new ways of expressing the classical Christology of Chalcedon in such a way that the "defects" of traditional school Christology can be avoided. Rahner tries to achieve this via his theological anthropology by which he develops an understanding of man in which the Hypostatic Union can take place without compromising the human nature of Jesus in any way. Indeed, from this synthetic presentation, we shall see that the humanity of Christ is the key factor in all of Rahner's theology. The Incarnation consistently plays a role in his theological writings. The reality of the human nature of Christ and its active, functional role in the economy of salvation are two of his insights which bear directly on the Devotion to the Sacred Heart. The presentation of Rahner's Christology in this chapter is necessarily limited.

We do not seek to duplicate the work of others, nor do we present an exhaustive study. This second chapter, however, represents a necessary step in the process of the thesis, because it sets the stage for the third chapter.

Chapter III is an attempt to verify the foundation and the content of Rahner's explanation of the symbol of the Heart of Jesus in reference to his Christology. Here it will be shown that the symbol and the Christology mutually condition and exegete one another. The emphasis which Rahner places on the perdurance of the humanity of Jesus and its active, functional relationship in the economy of salvation provides the foundation for the legitimacy of the symbol of the Heart of Christ.

Furthermore, it will be seen that certain of Rahner's insights from Christology help to clarify and make explicit many of his statements about the content of the symbol of the Heart of Christ. From this presentation it will become clear that one cannot understand and appreciate what Rahner says about the symbol of the Heart of Christ and its devotional realization unless one sees those statements against the specific background of his Christological thought. Despite the often abstract and speculative nature of Rahner's Christology, one misses the point entirely if one does not see that it opens the way to a prayerful and adoring relationship to the humanity of Jesus, such as the Devotion to the Sacred Heart proposes. This opening to prayer is not something extrinsic to Christology. It is entirely to be expected. The second half of Chapter III addresses the Christology of the "later" Rahner. Here we will briefly and schematically present Rahner's attempt to develop a "Christology from below." After presenting a critique of this attempt, we will address the question of whether, and how, this new Christological viewpoint can relate to the symbol of the Heart of Jesus. Here we will see that there are indeed elements in a Christology from below which are capable of being related to the symbol of the Heart of Christ as Rahner understands it. The incorporation of those elements in the practice of the Devotion today would be one way of contributing to attempts at updating the Devotion. Implicit in Chapter III are some relationships between theology and spirituality, at least in as much as that relationship exists in the framework of Rahner's thought.

Chapter IV, the conclusion of the thesis, is an explication of the relationship between theology and spirituality as it has been implicitly illustrated in the thesis, especially in Chapter III.

These conclusions are brief and could be understood as principles that apply both to spirituality and to theology. These "principles" are themselves in need of explication, and each of them could be developed at much greater length as topics for further research.

Throughout the presentation of the thesis I have used a numbering system to designate the sections of each chapter. I hope this contributes to clarifying the development of the argumentation in each section of the thesis. Most of Rahner's writings are topical articles. In order to present a unified picture of his thought, one must impose one's own structure on the body of Rahner's work. The numbering system, and the title of each section, are intended to make evident the structure which I have developed to organize the material.

THE HEART OF CHRIST IN THE WRITINGS OF KARL RAHNER

1.0. INTRODUCTION

In the first chapter, we propose to present an exposition of Rahner's thought on the Devotion to the Sacred Heart. This exposition will follow two basic steps: first, a presentation of Rahner's thought on symbolism in general; and second, the role of the symbol of the Heart of Christ in the Devotion to the Sacred Heart in particular. This exposition will then be followed by a summary of Rahner's thought on the Devotion to the Sacred Heart. This exposition will include a discussion of Rahner's though in light of his critics.

1.1.0. SYMBOLISM IN RAHNER: INTRODUCTION

In our exposition of Rahner's thought on symbolism we shall follow the same path which he himself takes in his writings, i.e., we shall proceed from his analysis of human language as revelatory of multiple levels of meaning among which is the symbolic, to his reflection on the reality of symbolism in itself. [1]

---

[1] As with much of Rahner's thought, this analysis must be gleaned from many different articles, some of them not directly related to the topic of the Sacred Heart in itself. Chief among these for our present exposition are: *"Behold this Heart!* Preliminaries to a Theology of the Devotion to the Sacred Heart," *Theological Investigations* III (London: Darton, Longman and Todd, 1963), pp. 321-330. Hereafter referred to as "Preliminaries." "Priest and Poet," *Theological Investigations* III, pp. 294-317. "The Theology of the Symbol," *Theological Investigations* IV (London: Darton, Longman and Todd, 1966), pp. 221-252. "The Theological Meaning of the Veneration of the Sacred Heart," *Theological Investigations* VIII (London: Darton, Longman and Todd, 1971), pp. 217-228. Hereafter cited as "Theological Meaning."

1.1.1.0. THE LINGUISTIC EXPERIENCE OF SYMBOLS: PRIMORDIAL
         WORDS

As with most of his contemporaries, Rahner begins his
analysis of symbolism with a phenomenological investigation of
human language, since it is in the experience of language that
man has his most immediate contact with the world of symbols.
Rahner begins this discussion with a distinction between *word*
and *concept*. The word has as its characteristics the notion of
corporeality, a figurative sense and concreteness, as distinct from
the concept with its abstract and universal characteristics. [2] In
his analysis, Rahner is using *word* in this concrete and corporeal
sense.

When we analyze how we use words, we discover that they
have many levels of meaning. When the scientist, for example,
speaks of water in the sense of a molecule of H_2O he means
something different from the poet. And certainly man's experience of the given reality of water is far richer than the chemist's
analytical molecule is capable of expressing.

> ... the water which is seen by man, praised by the poet and
> used in baptism by the Christian, is not a poetic glorification
> of the chemist's "water," as though he were the true realist;
> on the contrary, the "water" of the chemist is a narrowed down,
> technified and secondary derivative of the water of mankind. [3]

Water is but one example of a class of words whose meaning
is not exhausted by an essential definition. Among other words
of this kind Rahner mentions star, night, lightning, and blood. [4]
This experience of language leads Rahner to propose a distinction between two kinds of words: *utility words* and *primordial
words* (German: *Urworte*). Utility words are words which man
manufactures in order to name the things he experiences in his
intercourse with the world. They are univocal words whose
meaning is exhausted by the thing they define. Primordial words,
on the other hand, are words which by their very nature name a
reality which can never be exhausted by such an essential definition. They bear within them whole levels of experience and

---

[2] Rahner, "Preliminaries," *TI* III, p. 321f. This distinction has its
basis in Rahner's metaphysics of human knowing as proposed in his
work *Geist in Welt* (München: Kösel Verlag, 1957). For purposes of our
present discussion we will accept the distinction.

[3] *Ibid.*, p. 322.

[4] Rahner, "Priest and Poet," *TI* III, p. 298.

relationship which go beyond the simple naming of a thing.[5]
This distinction, however, is not one which can be imposed *a
priori* on all words. The distinction is based upon the experience
of the effect which certain words have upon us, an experience
which Rahner calls their "destiny."[6] Consequently, the distinction is only valid as long as these words *de facto* have this
destiny, and the class of primordial words changes with time.

On the basis of what Rahner says about these primordial
words, we can abstract the following characteristics of this class
of words :

1) They name a class of fundamental "givens" in human experience which seem to be given with nature, in distinction
   to man's creative action upon nature. At least in the examples
   which Rahner gives, primordial words express things or relationships which are, therefore, universal and are not limited
   by cultural or technological development.
2) Primordial words express things or relationships which are
   evocative of a multiplicity of subjective reactions within
   man. In this sense, while they name objective realities, they
   can never be limited in their *meaning* to these objective
   realities and still retain their *primordial* characteristic.
3) Given this multiplicity of primordial words, they nevertheless
   grasp man in such a way that their fundamental unity is
   never lost.
4) It is precisely this characteristic of the dialectic between unity
   and multiplicity which gives them their power and attrac-
   tion over man, because in the experience of the things of
   this world which he names with primordial words, he experiences himself as a fundamental unity who finds himself
   only in the multiplicity of the world.

1.1.1.1. *Heart as Primordial Word*

For Rahner, *heart* is a primordial word:

> "Heart" in its original ... meaning is a primordial word (Urwort):
> it is not susceptible of a proper definition by the logical com-
> position of "better known" concepts, and it is a word which ...

---

[5] *Ibi.*, p. 295ff.; "Preliminaries," *TI* III, p. 322; "Theological Meaning," *TI* VIII, p. 220f.
   [6] Rahner, "Preliminaries," *TI* III, p. 322; "Priest and Poet," *TI* III,
p. 296.

is so common to many cultures ... that in this sense too it may
be described as a primordial word, so that it can easily be
used in the vocabulary of a world religion.[7]

Heart has this property, however, completely apart from any
usage in religious language precisely because of the wealth of
meaning which it has in its natural usage. We have only to
look at the Scriptures, for example, to find a whole anthropology
in which the heart (*leb, lebab, kardia*) is seen as the center of
man's emotional, intellectual and moral life. It is viewed as
the central core of a man, the principle of his thoughts and
actions, the seat of his personality, his personal center. Because
heart has this natural meaning in Semitic anthropology, it could
be used so fruitfully in specifically religious applications, as e. g.,
Jer 9:22ff., where true allegiance to the Covenant is seen not
in terms of external circumcision, but in the true circumcision
of the heart. While such usage of the word heart was prevalent
in Semitic anthropology, and even though we have a different
anthropological viewpoint, our own modern languages retain
many expressions where the word heart or its root and deriva-
tives are used to express the same kind of personal center and
interiority.[8]

In calling heart a primordial word, Rahner insists that as
such, it can never mean only the muscular organ which pumps
blood through the body. Any such crassly physiological understanding of the word is as much an impoverishment of its true
meaning as H_2O is for water.

As with all words, "heart" does in fact name a specific object,
namely, a physical organ of the body. And yet without losing
this meaning and specific reference, it also always transports
man to a real experience of his personal being in radical unity.
For in knowing himself, man knows that he is a being of many
dimensions. The interiority of his conscious life and the action
of the world upon him; the exteriority of his action upon the

---

[7] Rahner, "Some Theses for a Theology of Devotion to the Sacred
Heart," *TI* III, pp. 331f. Hereafter cited as "Theses."
[8] For a complete overview of the use of the heart in the Scriptures
and in ancient literature in general, cf. P. Dhorme, *L'emploi metaphori-
que des noms de parties du corps en hébreu et en akkadien*, Paris, 1923;
A. Guillaumant, "Les sens des noms du coeur dans l'antiquité" in *Le
Coeur*: Etudes Carmélitaines (Toulouse: Desclée de Brouwer, 1950), pp. 41-
81; F. Baumgaertl and J. Behm, "Kardia," in *TDNT* III, ed. G. Kittel
(Grand Rapids: Eerdmans, 1965), pp. 605-613.

world; his experience of himself as source and the "otherness" of what springs from that source; his experience of things as central or peripheral to his life — these and a variety of similar experiences confront man with himself as a mystery:

> A form of knowledge which is faced with the mystery of the unity in multiplicity, of being in appearance, of the whole in the part and the part in the whole, and utters primordial words which are designed precisely to evoke this mystery, is difficult to grasp and dark, like the reality itself which gains mastery over us in such words and draws us into its incomprehensible depths. In primordial words of this kind spirit and flesh, meaning and its symbol, concept and word, object and image are still originally one (which does not mean they are simply the same).[9]

And so man searches for a word to define this original experience of his unity in the radical multiplicity of his life. It is this interior unity of his person that man calls "heart." It is this experience, this mystery of his own being which is evoked and which grasps man every time he uses the word heart.[10]

> For the moment we mention the term "heart" even in quite general terms, and even apart from the religious dimension ... we are referring not to one factor among many others, nor even simply to all things in their diversity as drawn together into a subsequent unity. We are referring rather to an interior centre from which the diversification of human reality is unfolded and in which this diversification, which also belongs to the very nature of man, remains united.[11]

For Rahner, the heart is the personal center of man. The discovery that he has a heart is the discovery of "one of the crucial secrets of his existence."[12] However, this discovery is a confrontation with the ambivalence of his humanity, for in the discovery of the personal center of his heart, man also discovers that it is a personal center capable of both love and hate. Thus the heart is not immediately evocative of only love. But man is aware that all his attitudes are "cordial" in the sense that they arise from the center of his being which is his heart.[13]

---

[9] Rahner, "Preliminaries," *TI* III, p. 331f.
[10] *Ibid.*, p. 325f.
[11] Rahner, "Preliminaries," *TI* III, p. 323.
[12] *Ibid.*, p. 326, and "Theses," *TI* III, pp. 333-335.
[13] "Preliminaries," *TI* III, p. 327.

Of this personal center, the physical heart of man is "a genuine, original symbol, a primordial symbol (Ursymbol)." [14]

When Rahner writes of the heart as a symbol he is indirectly preparing the ground for a discussion of the meaning of the Heart of Christ as the object of the devotion to the Sacred Heart. Again we will follow the route which Rahner himself takes in this discussion, and so we continue with his ontology of symbolism.

1.1.2.0. THE ONTOLOGICAL BASIS OF SYMBOLISM

Rahner begins his ontology of symbolism with the observation that both in its history and in its contemporary understanding the word symbol is used to denote the ability of one being to represent another, either because of some inherent agreement between the two, or because of some relationship or association in the mind of the observer. This understanding of symbol has an etymological basis in the word itself. However, Rahner is quick to point out that such a starting point as the word "symbol" itself might yield is inadequate, first because it can equally apply to both true symbols and merely conventional signs, and second, because it does not seem to adequately explain the experience of true symbols. Therefore, he rejects this etymological, superficial understanding of symbolism as the starting point for his discussion.[15]

While admitting the provisional character of what he has to say, Rahner insists that the starting point for a true understanding of symbolism must be sought in the principles of a general ontology. He defines the purpose of his search as follows:

> Our task will be to look for the highest and most primordial manner in which one reality can represent another — considering the matter from the formal ontological point of view. And we call this supreme and primal representation, in which one reality renders another present (primarily "for itself" and only secondarily for others), a symbol: the representation which allows the other "to be there." [16]

---

[14] Rahner, "Unity, Love, Mystery," *TI* VIII, p. 230.

[15] Rahner, "The Theology of the Symbol," *TI* IV, p. 224f. This is one of Rahner's most original and difficult articles. In some instances the English translation is inaccurate. Where this occurs I will quote my own version in the text, and the German original as well as the translation from *Theological Investigations* in the footnote.

[16] *Ibid.*, p. 225.

With this task in mind, then, Rahner proceeds to his first statement of an ontology of symbolism.

> Our first statement, which we put forward as the basic principle of an ontology of symbolism is as follows: *all beings are by their nature symbolic, because they necessarily "express" themselves in order to attain their own nature.*[17]

The demonstration of this statement involves the discussion of two main points: the unity and multiplicity of being, and the emanation of the faculties of the soul from the being of the soul itself, which St. Thomas calls resultant causality.

1.1.2.1. *The Unity and Multiplicity of Being*

Rahner begins his demonstration by stating that his starting point is the fact "that a being (i.e., each one) is multiple *in se* and that in this unity of the multiple, one [aspect] in this multiplicity is or can be essentially an expression of another [aspect] in this multiple unity."[18] For Rahner, the first clause of this statement is self-evident as regards finite beings, since their lack of simplicity is precisely what makes them finite. This may be taken as a general principle of Scholastic ontology.[19] But Rahner insists that there is a sense in which multiplicity and differentiation can be understood not only in a negative sense

---

[17] *Ibid.*, p. 224. Italics mine.

[18] Rahner, "Zur Theologie des Symbols," *Schriften* IV, p. 279f. The translation is my own. The German text reads: "Um einer ursprünglichen Begriff des Symbols zu erreichen, müssen wir davon ausgehen, daß ein Seiendes (d.h. jedes) in sich plural ist und in dieser Einheit des Pluralen — eines in dieser Pluralität wesentlich Ausdruck eines anderen in dieser pluralen Einheit ist oder sein kann." In Footnote 5 on the same page Rahner notes that his use of the word "eines" is deliberately vague; but that it refers to one moment in a composite being is clear. Rahner continues in the Footnote that the oneness of this moment must be understood analogously to the oneness and completeness of the being itself. The translation of this sentence in *Theological Investigations* IV, p. 225f., reads as follows: "To reach the primary concept of symbol, we must start from the fact that all beings (each of them, in fact) are multiple, and are or can be essentially the expression of another in this unity of the multiple and one in this plurality, by reason of its plural unity." To say the least, this translation is inadequate because it obfuscates the main point, namely, that in a composite being one of the elements has the possibility of being the original symbol of the whole or of one of the other elements.

[19] Cf., e.g., *Summa Theologica* I, 3.1-8.

as the lack of the perfection of simplicity, but rather in a positive sense, as a general characteristic of all being, including God. He does this by introducing into a general ontology a theological datum: the Trinity. When we take into consideration that through revelation and faith the Absolute of ontology becomes the Personal God of the Divine Trinity, then we can say "that there is a true and real — even though 'only' relative — distinction of 'persons' in the supreme simplicity of God, and hence a plurality, at least in this sense." [20] A further step leads us to a consideration of the relationship between finite beings and God. If we consider God as Exemplary Cause of all that is, then we can say that the multiplicity of finite beings must not be considered as a merely negative quality of their finitude. Rather this multiplicity could also be seen as a reflection or result of the divine multiplicity, considered as the highest perfection of Being as Rahner understands it when applied to God. Thus Rahner concludes that the first part of his statement that "being is multiple *in se*" can be understood as a general principle of ontology.[21]

Two further questions remain to be asked. First, how do these two elements of unity and multiplicity relate to one another in one and the same being? And secondly, how does being express itself, and is this self-expression of being of such a nature that one of the plurality of constitutive elements of that being can be its primary symbol?

In the order of being, when faced with the reality of a composite being, primacy must be given either to the multiplicity of acts and forms of operation, or to the unity of the being whose acts and forms these are. Or to state the problem in another way, as Rahner does: is the unity of a being merely the sum and composite of its differentiated acts and operations, or is the unity of a being the principle from which these acts and operations proceed? [22] True multiplicity is constituted by real differentiation and distinction of acts. But true multiplicity cannot be the principle of the unity of a being, as Rahner points out in quoting "the profound principle of St. Thomas: *non enim plura secundum se uniuntur.*" [23] The real differentiation which is experienced in the multiplicity of a being must be understood

---

[20] Rahner, "Theology of the Symbol," *TI* IV, p. 226.
[21] *Ibid.*, p. 226f.
[22] *Ibid.*, p. 227.
[23] *Ibid.*, p. 227.

as the self-realization and self-expression of the original unity of that being.

Rahner reintroduces the fact of the Trinity to point out that the tension between the unity and multiplicity of being must not necessarily be understood as a negative quality of being.

> A consideration of the Trinity shows that the "one" of unity and plurality, thus understood, is an ontological ultimate, which may not be reduced to an abstract and merely apparently "higher" unity and simplicity: it cannot be a hollow, lifeless identity. It would be theologically a heresy, and therefore ontologically an absurdity, to think that God would be really "simpler" and hence more perfect, if there were no real distinction of persons in God.[24]

On the basis of this argumentation Rahner concludes that being as such reaches its perfection by achieving its own plurality. This plurality, however, must always be understood as having its origin in the original unity of being (*ens* as *unum*). The plurality of distinct moments of a being always bears the mark of the original unity, sincc this unity is the foundation of the plural moments; and the plural moments are the means by which the original unity reaches its proper self-perfection.[25] The relationship of unity and multiplicity, then, is a relationship of *originans* and *originatum*.[26] The unity of a being diversifies itself in order to realize itself; the individual moments of this diversified unity always bear the mark of the original unity within them.

The clarification of this relationship enables us to proceed to the second part of Rahner's statement: "in this unity of the multiple, one [aspect] is or can be essentially an expression of another [aspect] in this multiple unity."[27] Here we are dealing with the question of how being expresses itself. The answer to this question will enable us to come to the primary understanding of symbol which is the goal of this present section.

---

[24] *Ibid.*, p. 227f.

[25] *Ibid.*, p. 228.

[26] I have borrowed this terminology from the theology of original sin, since it seems to best express the relationship which Rahner is trying to explain.

[27] Cf. *supra*, p. 25.

1.1.2.2. The "Expressiveness" of Being

Thus far we have seen that in the sense in which Rahner has stated it, the statement "Being is multiple *in se*" may be taken as a general principle of ontology. This means that every being achieves its own self-fulfillment in and through a process of differentiation. By positing its own "other," being realizes itself. This "other" bears the mark of its origin in the unity of the being.

Rahner now argues that this "other" is the primary expression of the being. The positing of this "other" is the condition of the possibility of presence to the world (knowability) and of possession of self in knowledge and love (being known). And since the degree of knowing and being known is the primary indication of the degree of the possession of being (*In tantum est ens cognoscens et cognitum, in quantum est ens actu*), we may conclude that the differentiation of being is the condition of the posibility of realizing itself. To the degree that a being expresses itself in its differentiated other, to that degree it possesses being; and to the degree that it possesses being, to that dgree it makes itself known and possesses itself in knowledge and love.[28]

Rahner's argumentation here is very schematic. He refers the reader to *Geist in Welt,* and since the argumentation there is much clearer, we will adduce an example from that work to make the reasoning clear. In that work [29] Rahner discusses the role of sensibility in human knowledge. For man to know an object it must first be present to his senses; to be present to his senses the object must be a material object capable of acting upon man's senses. Now what is the nature of material being? It is composed of prime matter and substantial form. But these two together, while constituting the essence of the object, cannot be known until the object is differentiated. This differentiation takes place first of all with the giving of the form of *quantity*. Only when prime matter and substantial form are differentiated by the accidental form of quantity, whereby the being receives extension and hence its own distinction from other objects of the same essence, can *this* being be known as a distinct object.

But quantity (extension) is not known in and for itself either.

---

[28] Rahner, "The Theology of the Symbol," *TI* IV, pp. 228-234.
[29] Cf. K. Rahner, *Geist in Welt* (München: Kösel Verlag, 1957), pp. 91-128.

A further process of differentiation is required and is achieved through the accidental forms of quality. It is the qualities that are perceived on a sense level as the proper object of the senses. Thus the object is known because its qualities are known; in the act of knowing the qualities there is the perception of quantity; and because the object is quantified it can be known as an object-for-itself. This process of differentiation, then, is seen as the condition of the possibility of knowledge of this object. This process leads to the formation of the *species sensibilis*, which is, in its turn, the condition of the possibility of intellectual knowledge.

Thus we can see that the process by which the unity of a being is differentiated to form its own plurality is the process by which being makes itself present to the world. It is by this process of differentiaton that a being forms its own *species* and thus expresses itself to the world.

1.1.2.3. *Resultance (Resultantia)*

St. Thomas sees an analogous development and differentiation of the soul itself.[30] Upon informing the body the soul has fulfilled its function as substantial form. How then do the powers of the soul relate to the soul itself? Are they really distinct accidents, or is the essence of the soul its powers? St. Thomas insists that the soul cannot be identified with its powers, that they are really distinct from the soul as accidents are really distinct from substance. But since the soul is simple, the traditional categories of substance-accident and the usual modes of causality are not sufficient to express the relationship between the soul and its powers. Hence, St. Thomas uses the word "resultance" to describe this relationship. The notion is undeveloped, but its meaning is clear. The powers of the soul flow one from another, but according to a double mode. In the order of substance the intellective powers provide the finality for the sensitive powers, and the sensitive powers provide the finality for the nutritive powers. All three inhere in the one subject by virtue of their inherence in the soul. But in the order of material development, this differentiation takes place in the opposite order, i.e., first the nutritive powers develop, then the sensitive, then the intellective. For Thomas, this differentiation is given, at least in potency, with the giving of the soul itself,

---

[30] Cf. *Summa Theologica*, I, 77, 6 ad 3; 77, 7.

and this prior to any distinct actuation of powers in "second act." Thus in a real sense the soul expresses itself by differentiating itself in an immanent act of self-realization which is prior to any secondary, transient activity.

Rahner refers to this Thomist teaching as a further indication of the validity of his first statement, namely, that all being expresses itself and its unity in a process of differentiation. The importance of this Thomist teaching for the further development of Rahner's argumentation will be seen below. Its purpose is to further strengthen his position that all being, even simple being such as God or the soul of man, realizes itself by a process of differentiating its unity.[31]

1.1.2.4. *Being as Symbolic*

For Rahner, then, all being is by its very nature symbolic because all being, in the process of realizing itself, differentiates its original and essential unity by forming its own "other." In and through this "other", being expresses itself, primarily to itself, secondarily for others. This "other" is the *eidos* and *morphe* of Greek philosophy; it is the *species* of the Scholastics. This "other" which is the differentiated self-expression of the unity of a being is its primary symbol, its *Ursymbol*. Thus symbolism has its foundation *not* in the representation of one thing by another, *nor* in the ability of an observer to note some similarity between two things. Rather, symbolism has its foundation in the very nature of being itself.

1.1.2.5. *Theological Implications*

It remains for us now to work out the theological implicatons of this ontological understanding of symbol. Rahner himself accomplishes this by referring to four areas of theology, namely, the Trinity, Christology, Sacraments and Eschatology. We will briefly treat each of these areas in order to arrive at some clarifications that will bear directly on the heart as symbol in the devotion to the Heart of Christ.

1) *Trinity*

The mystery of the Trinity has already played a role in this discussion on symbolism. Rahner sees it as an indication

---

[31] "Theology of the Symbol," *TI* IV, pp. 232-234.

of the truth of his ontological principle of symbolism.   In this
theological context he specifies how the ontology applies to God.
The generation of the Logos in the inner-trinitarian processions
is the highest form of symbolism in the sense in which Rahner
has defined his terms.   "The Logos is the 'word' of the Father,
his perfect 'image,' his 'imprint,' his radiance, his self-expression." [32]   Two points of traditional theology help to clarify this
statement.   First, the Father generates the Word as his own
image and expression.   Second, this generation is "necessarily
given with the divine act of self-knowledge, and without it the
absolute act of divine self-possession in knowledge cannot exist." [33]   To state this in the terms used above, we may say that
the Father becomes himself, realizes his personality as Father,
inasmuch as he generates the Word.   This Word is the perfect
self-expression of the Father, of the same essence and divine substance, and yet really other.

> But this means that the Logos is the "symbol" of the Father, in
> the very sense we have given the word: the inward symbol
> which remains distinct from what is symbolized, which is con-
> stituted by what is symbolized, where what is symbolized ex-
> presses itself and possesses itself.[34]

2) Christology [35]

Rahner states that the doctrine of the Incarnation is the
obvious core of any theology of symbolism.   But certain ways
of thought must be avoided if we are to appreciate the meaning
of this central Christian symbol.   For the true *symbolic* meaning of the humanity of Christ must be allowed to play its role
in our discussion.   If we understand humanity in the well-known
sense in which we use it of ourselves, and if we then predicate
humanity of Christ in a static way as something which he
"assumes" or takes on, then this humanity has been reduced
to the "function" of a signal or a uniform, but would have no
intrinsic relationship with the Logos.   The humanity would be
a sign, but not a symbol in the true sense of the word.   Jesus
Christ as the revelation of the Father in the Son cannot be pro-

---

[32] *Ibid.,* p. 236.
[33] *Ibid.,* p. 236.
[34] *Ibid.,* p. 236.
[35] Many of these themes will be developed in our second chapter.
They are merely touched upon here in order to demonstrate the thrust of
Rahner's thought.

perly conceived as having a humanity in order that *verba* and *facta* might be made known in history. This would make his humanity an extrinsic means of revelation. Rather Jesus Christ must be conceived as the revelation of the Father in the Son *in his humanity itself.* Only thus can the humanity have a proper function as symbol by really making present in and through itself that which it symbolizes.[36]

The implications of this are far reaching. For now, in light of the Incarnation, the symbolic character of being has been given a new dimension. No longer is being symbolic merely for itself, nor merely in its ability to transport man via a natural transcendence to God. By virtue of the Incarnation the symbolic reality of all being has received "an infinite extension" because it "has become ... a determination of the Logos himself or of his milieu." [37] This is one of the most important foundations for the legitimacy of using the symbol of the Heart in a Christological devotion.

3) *Sacraments*

Rahner mentions that the classic place for the use of a theology of the symbol is the Sacraments. But he mentions that the notion of symbolism achieved in this study provides new insights into the classical axioms of sacramental theology. For this idea of symbolism shows that the causality of grace in sacramental signs cannot be put into merely physical or moral terms. Thus this idea of symbolism enables theology to transcend those categories by showing that the grace itself is symbolically present in the sign. "In a word, the grace of God constitutes itself actively present in the sacraments by creating their expression, their historical tangibility in space and time, which is its own symbol." [38]

4) *Eschatology*

It could be thought that Eschatology would be the teaching on the final removal of symbols, of the immediacy of the vision of God. But this absolute immediacy is never achieved. For

---

[36] Whole paragraph, cf. "Theology of the Symbol," *TI* IV, pp. 236-240. Rahner does not claim that anyone actually *says* that Jesus' humanity is only a sign. It is, however, an "effective presupposition" of some Christologies. Cf. p. 238.

[37] *Ibid.*, p. 239.

[38] *Ibid.*, p. 242.

in order to enjoy the *visio beata* man needs the *lumen gloriae* as the mediation to immediacy. And for this *lumen gloriae*, since it is a supernatural grace, the humanity of Christ must retain its mediating function. This once again shows the Incarnation as the most fundamental Christian symbol. Many other symbols will pass away, but this one will remain.[39]

5) *Two Principles for a Theology of Symbolism*

We conclude this consideration of the theological meaning of symbolism by simply quoting the two principles which Rahner has developed on the basis of these considerations:

> ... the concept of symbol ... is an essential key-concept in all theological treatises, without which it is impossible to have a correct understanding of the subject-matter of the various treatises in themselves and in relation to other treatises.
>   The principle that God's salvific action on man, from its first foundations to its completion, always takes place in such a way that God himself is the reality of salvation, because it is given to man and grasped by him in the symbol, which does not represent an absent and merely promised reality but exhibits this reality as something present by means of the symbol formed by it.[40]

1.1.2.6. *Summary*

This analysis of Rahner's thought on the ontology and theology of symbolism has brought us to the point where we can begin now to speak of the meaning of the symbol of the heart. On the ontological level we now have to retrace our steps a bit to judge the authenticity of the symbol of the heart as it is used to express the totality of a person's interiorty as it relates to the world. This, in effect, must answer the question of whether — and how — one organ of the body, which is itself only part of the whole man, can be used to express and make present the whole totality of a person. For these indeed are the criteria which emerge from the ontological discussion: the formation of the symbol as the co-natural expression of the process of the self-realization of being (authenticity of the symbol); the ability of the symbol to make really present, first to itself and then to others, the being of that which it is the

---

[39] *Ibid.*, p. 244.
[40] *Ibid.*, p. 245.

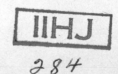

symbol (functionality of the symbol). This critique of the symbol of the heart will provide us with a solid *anthropological* basis for the use of the heart in the devotion.

1.1.3.0. HEART AS PRIMORDIAL SYMBOL

We must now apply the criteria of symbolism to the heart. We proceed here in two steps by asking: first, what possible justification can there be for symbolizing a person, who is essentially a spiritual-material reality, by using one part of the material aspect of that person (the question of the *authenticity* of the symbol); second, does heart, as one part of the material reality of a person, actually smbolize the person (the question of the *functionality* of the symbol).

1.1.3.1. *The Authenticity of the Symbol*

One could answer the first question simply by assuming the fact of man's symbolic activity, by simply referring to the fact that man uses this symbol of the heart in his language, literature and art to express the fulness of his personhood. This assumption seeks no further explanation for this fact. But this would leave us on a superficial level with no understanding of the reason why we speak this way and the implications of this linguistic and artistic fact. If we wish to go further in our consideration of the heart as symbol, then we must ask the ontological question.

Rahner seeks to make this contribution to the discussion by interpreting St. Thomas' teaching on the relationship of the body and soul in man in terms of the body as the symbol of the soul, and hence of the whole person. For St. Thomas the intellectual soul is the substantial form of the body.[41]

---

[41] Cf. *Summa Theologica* I, 76. The whole of Question 76 deals with the union of the soul with the body. Thomas develops his argument from a variety of points of view in eight parts.

First, he asks whether the intellective principle in man is united to the body as its form. Here Thomas treats the question of how an essentially spiritual reality can be the form of a material thing.

Second, Thomas asks whether there are as many intellective principles as there are human bodies. Here he speaks of the principle of individuation of souls and rejects the argument, based on the fact that all men know the same universal forms, that there is only one intellective principle for all men.

Rahner interprets this specifically Thomistic teaching on the body-soul relationship in terms of his own theory of symbolism. Thus the body is the symbol of the soul. Rahner reasons to this conclusion first, from the real distinction between body and soul, and secondly, from their mutual relationship in the one man. The first point, the real distinction between body and soul, is general Scholastic teaching. But the explanation of the relationship between them in terms of prime matter and substan-

---

Third, he asks whether there is more than one soul in man, i.e., are there distinct nutritive and sensitive souls in man besides the intellective soul. Here Thomas argues for the unicity of the soul in man, one intellective-spiritual soul which contains the powers of nutrition and sensation.

Fourth, Thomas asks whether there is any other form in man besides the intellective soul. Here he is addressing and rejecting the idea of a *forma corporeitatis* which informs the body prior to its being informed by the intellective soul.

Fifth, Thomas addresses the question of the suitability of the intellective soul to be united with a material body. He answers this question by insisting that matter exists for form, and not the other way around. Matter, as prime matter, is purely passive potency with regard to its substantial act. Thomas argues from the intellect's need for and dependence upon sensation to prove this point. The intellect needs sensation, and hence organs of sense, and thus a material body. Thus the question of suitability must be answered by starting with the form and not the matter.

Sixth, Thomas asks whether there must be some mediating accidental disposition of the body in order to prepare it for its unification with the soul. Thomas responds in the negative, relying on the distinction between substantial and accidental forms. There can be no accidental form without the prior act of existence. But existence comes from the union of prime matter and substantial form. Hence substantial form is prior to accidental form both logically and chronologically. Thus there can be no accidental form or disposition of matter which is prior to that matter's having real existence due to its substantial form.

Having ruled out the mediation of accidental forms, of a *forma corporeitatis* and of other souls, Thomas asks in the seventh place whether there is some *material* disposition or mediation to the union of soul and body. Thomas answers in the negative and rejects the theories of mediation through breath, light or other such media.

Finally, in the eighth place, Thomas asks whether the whole soul is in every part of the body. There are apparent reasons for rejecting this notion. If the whole soul were in each part of the body, then each part would have existence for itself and not as part of an organism; or each organ would possess all the soul's powers; or there would be no hierarchy of organic parts. Thomas rejects these objections and insists that, since the soul is united to the body as its substantial form, it is whole in the whole and whole in every part. Thomas proves this by the fact that no part of the body retains its activity once the soul has left

tial form is uniquely Thomist. Rahner, drawing out the implications of Thomas' explanation, shows that the body, as prime
matter, has no real existence as *body* without the soul, to which
it has a purely passive relationship. Thus the organization and
actualization of the body is completely dependent upon the
action of the soul, as substantial form, on the body. Rahner
concludes that in the Thomist theory of the relationship, all the
criteria for saying that the body is the symbol of the soul are
present: *first*, the soul, by its information of prime matter,
posits it as its own really distinct "other," namely, a human
body; *second*, the body, as that which is posited, is an instrinsic
part of the being, "man," which is thus constituted; *third*, in
this process the soul realizes its own intrinsic nature as informing principle, and expresses itself by the exercise of its informing presence upon the whole body and by the operation of its
powers through the various parts of that body.[42]   Thus Rahner

---

the body. Further, and important for our discussion, he distinguishes between quantitative, essential, and potential (or virtual) wholeness. Since
quantitative wholeness is accidental, it does not apply to our discussion.
The other two types do. The whole soul is in the whole body essentially,
because it constitutes with the body the essence of man. However, there
is a different kind of relationship when we speak of powers of the soul
as present in specific organs of the body. Here the relationship is that
of "parts," i.e., organs of the body and specific powers of the soul con-
nected with them, to the "whole," i.e., the one man. However, it is the
whole presence of the soul in those parts which makes them to be precisely parts of the whole.

Thus in Question 76 Thomas has demonstrated that the soul is the
substantial form of the body. Thus the soul gives the body existence, all
its faculties and powers, and establishes a hierarchical order among the
various organs of the body. It does this *immediately*, by virtue of its
essence and its powers, by its informing presence in the body. In closing
this discussion of Question 76 and before proceeding to Rahner's use of
Thomas' insight, a quote from this Question will help us to see where this
discussion is leading:

> One part of the body is said to be more important than another
> because of the various powers of which the parts of the body are
> the organs. The organ of the most important power, or even the
> organ which most serves that power, is the most important organ.

Summa Theologica I, 76, 8 ad 5. Orig: Ad quintum dicendum est quod
una pars corporis dicitur esse principalior quam alia propter potentias
diversas quarum sunt organa partes corporis. Quae enim est principalioris
potentiae organum est principalior pars corporis; vel quae etiam eidem
potentiae principalius deservit. English translation taken from *Summa
Theologiae*, v. XI, "Man," transl. Timothy Suttor (London: Blackfriars,
1970), p. 87.

[42] Cf. Rahner, "The Theology of the Symbol," *TI* IV, pp. 245ff.

has established the basis for allowing the material part of a material-spiritual composite to be the symbol of an essentially spiritual reality, the soul.[43]

But now this generalized concept must be applied specifically to the question of how one part, one organ, of a complex material-spiritual organism can be used to symbolize the whole. Establishing the basis for this kind of symbolis usage will establish the authenticity of the heart as symbol.

Rahner proceeds to this specification by a further reflection on the teaching of St. Thomas. First there is the teaching that the whole soul is in every part of the body in its essential totality. The vital presence of the soul in each and every part of the body is that which precisely makes those parts to be parts of *this* body. Thus the body is not merely a *quantitative* whole made up of individual parts. It is rather an *essential* whole, which means that each of the parts is engaged in the activity of the whole.[44] Rahner adduces two examples to explain the meaning of this statement. When man speaks, the activity is limited to just a few organs of the body: lungs, larynx, tongue, palate and lips. Yet the whole man is present in his speech. When a man is ill, the illness is located in one or more of the organs of the body. Yet the illness affects the whole man as a psychosomatic unity. Rahner sees in these and similar examples the deeper meaning of the soul's information of the body:

> It is not just that the simple substantial principle of a quantitatively extended entity must be as a whole in every part of this entity. The assertion also means that this substantial "presence" of the soul implies that it determines and informs each part *as* part of the *whole*. And this once more cannot merely mean that the part is ordained, as regards its physiological function, to the service of the whole. It also implies that in a mysterious concentration of the symbolic function of the body, each part bears once more within itself the symbolic force and function of the whole, by contributing its part to the whole of the symbol.[45]

---

[43] Rahner himself states that there remains the question of the adequacy of the symbolic expression of the soul in the body. Thomas does not have these reservations and seems to argue for the adequacy of the body without any doubts. Cf. *Summa* I, 76, 5.

[44] Rahner, "The Theology of the Symbol," *TI* IV, p. 247. The distinction is based on *Summa* I, 76, 8.

[45] *Ibid.*, p. 248.

This in turn is a further indication of the truth of the ontological principle of symbolism which was the first assertion of this discussion. The "other" of primary symbolism is a *differentiated* other; the differentiation is a result of the self-realization of what is symbolized. When dealing with a simple being such as the soul, this necessarily means that, despite the differentiation process, the whole soul in its totality is present in each of the parts of the body. This does *not* mean, however, that each part is of equal value. There is a hierarchy of parts of the body, determined by the degree of necessity of the various organs "for the survival and perfection of the whole." [46] Rahner admits that one cannot make a case for the strict correspondence between the biological necessity and the symbolic function of the parts of the body. But that is not important of itself in this consideration. What is of primary importance here is to see the implications of this metaphysical discussion for the symbolic use of the parts of the body in human language. Precisely because they are differentiated parts of a whole which is itself the self-posited "other" of a more primary unified being, the use of the parts of the body in symbolic language

> does not signify only the part as such, that is, as a quantitative, material piece of the whole body; it always signifies the one whole, composed of the symbol-generating origin and the material piece of reality which, as portion of the whole, single and symbolic body, bears within it under a certain aspect the symbolic function of the whole body.[47]

Thus the heart can be used as an authentic symbol of the whole person, and its usage in the language of literature, love, and religion finds in this ontology its profound foundation, and this usage itself is an indication of the truth of the ontological principle.

1.1.3.2. *The Functionality of the Symbol*

The establishment of the metaphysical basis of the symbolism of the heart has established the condition of the possibility of its use as an authentic symbol. But this alone does not mean that it actually does function as such. Additional criteria are needed to make this kind of judgment.

---

[46] *Ibid.*, p. 249.
[47] *Ibid.*, p. 249.

There are many different claims made for symbolism, and many different viewpoints from which symbolism has been examined.[48] But for the sake of our presentation we have decided to use those characteristics of symbolism which are common to all these points of view, as criteria for judging whether or not something is truly operating on the level of symbol. Since there is little agreement as to the precise nature of symbolic activity, if we can show at least that the heart fulfills those functions which *are* agreed upon by most, we will have shown that the heart realizes the metaphysical possibility and actually does function as a symbol. Many of these criteria will coincide with Rahner's description of primordial words. Their inclusion here will help to broaden the discussion and provide the basis for a critique of Rahner's position.

We state the following five characteristics of symbols, based on analysis of their functioning:

1) Symbols are born, not manufactured, and hence have a certain natural quality;

2) Symbols are equivocal in meaning and hence are open to a variety of interpretations;

3) Symbols communicate meaning and value and hence are evocative of a response of commitment on both the internal and external levels;

4) Symbols give knowledge of reality via the direct rational *and* emotional experience of the thing symbolized;

5) Because of their equivocal nature, symbols are capable of corruption into signs.[49]

We will now apply these characteristics to the symbol of the heart to show that it does indeed function on the level of symbol.

1) A glance at the dictionary immediately will reveal the fact that the word "heart" has many meanings and uses.[50] Most

---

[48] E.g., as here, theological and philosophical. Others include artistic, literary, sociological and anthropological, and psychological.

[49] I have taken these five characteristics of symbols from three very diverse sources: theological, T. Fawcett, *The Symbolic Language of Religion* (London: SCM, 1970), pp. 26-39; anthropological, R. Firth, *Symbols: Public and Private* (Ithaca: Cornell University Press, 1973), pp. 15-91; comparative religions, M. Eliade, *Images and Symbols* (New York: Sheed and Ward, 1969), p. 12ff.

[50] Cf. *Websters New International Dictionary*, unabridged edition (Springfield, Mass.: 1958), p. 1150.

of these usages deal with the emotional and psychic activity of man. This symbolic usage of the word has as its basis the fact that the ancients of Egyptian, Semitic, Greco-Roman and the Inca civilizations considered the heart to be the place where these faculties are located.[51] This anatomical association is no longer accepted by contemporary man. And yet this symbolic usage persists. But this persistence should not be considered an anomaly, since both it and the outmoded anatomical explanation have their common basis in another fact, namely, that thought and volition give rise to emotional responses which do indeed affect the heart. Thus this usage of the word, despite all the advances of modern medical knowledge and technology, is not something which is kept alive artificially. Rather this usage expresses a natural occurrence in man.

2) An examination of the uses given in the dictionary also makes the equivocal meaning of the symbol evident. In a typically symbolic way of thought we find a *coincidentia oppositorum*, inasmuch as the heart can stand for good and evil, love and hate, hope and despair. Thus the reality conveyed by this symbol, while always referring to the innermost core of human, personal being, may refer to two completely opposite relationships.

3) The relationship conveyed by the symbol communicates meaning and value and thus evokes an internal and external response of commitment of some kind. Once the relationship conveyed by the symbol has been determined, there follows the communication of meaning and value inherent in the symbol. Thus once the symbol of the heart, as a symbol of the entire engagement of a man's personal forces, has been perceived to convey, e.g., love, there is the perception of the depth of personal involvement and the concomitant values of love. This in turn evokes the internal response of returning love and the external response of ordering one's acts accordingly. It is this quality of true symbols to evoke this kind of response that gives them their real operative power in man's life. The determination of meaning and value is often contingent upon social and cultural forces. Symbols can be manipulated by a society to function as a control factor for producing behavior acceptable to a society. Thus a religious society such as the Church determines for its own members the meaning and value of the symbols it uses

[51] Cf. Guillaumant's article in *Le Coeur*, op. cit.

and seeks to evoke internal responses (e.g., faith) and external responses (e.g., moral actions) which are appropriate to those symbols.

4) Symbols give knowledge via the direct rational *and* emotional experience of the thing symbolized. Thus the symbol of the heart, used to express the intensity of personal engagement in the act described, conveys knowledge both of the action and the degree of personal engagement. This in turn conveys a direct insight into the experience which is conveyed through the use of the symbol. An example will help to clarify this point. A person could express a desire to buy a Cadillac in two ways: "I want to buy a Cadillac," or "I want to buy a Cadillac with all my heart." Both statements convey knowledge of the desire, but only the second statement conveys directly the real experience of the desire itself which the person is experiencing, bcause he expresses it in terms which communicate via a symbol the total engament of his person in the desire.

5) Because of their equivocal nature, symbols are capable of corruption into signs. This happens when they cease to convey the meaning and value which they had originally. At that point the symbol must be refunctioned to convey a new set of meanings and values or it must die as a symbol and become a mere sign. Thus a heart carved on a tree with two sets of initials was originally meant to symbolize the love and affection which those two people have for one another. As long as this meaning and value is present, that heart stands as a symbol. But if that relationship should cease to exist, the heart ceases to have the function of symbol and becomes merely a sign that at some time or other in the past, those two people were in that place.

These examples demonstrate the functioning of the heart on the level of symbol. But now we must take up the specific criteria which Rahner develops in his theory of symbolism. These are the internal cohesion between the symbol and the symbolized, and the self-realization of the symbolized in the symbol. The first of Rahner's criteria, i.e., the internal cohesion between the symbol and the symbolized, coincides with the first of the five characteristics of symbols which we mentioned above, namely, that they are born, not manufactured. This is another way of stating the insight which led to the formulation of the ontological principle, because both are based in the experience of symbols. That experience is one of an immediate, natural connection between the symbol and the symbolized. It is not an artificial construct imposed upon the symbolic reality. Rather, the very nature of the symbol discloses what is symbolized. Thus man's interior psychic and emotional life is a series of formally immanent acts which affect him as a psychosomatic unity and determine his relationship to the world around him. Man's heart is one of the principle active organs in both of these actions, because it responds to emotional stimuli and increases its activity to enable the body to react. As such it is a natural symbol for man's psychic and emotional life which is at the core of human personality.

The second of Rahner's criteria covers the second, third and fourth characteristics of symbols, all of which deal with the knowledge and affective response communicated by the symbol. For Rahner, man realizes himself to the degree that he knows and wills.[52] As our discussion of the characteristics of symbols has pointed out, when man engages in symbolic activity he experiences the unity of knowledge and volition in a radical, albeit unthematic, way. Thus man uses the symbol of the heart to express the whole complex of psychic activities by which he knows and loves. In these activities he comes to know himself and to will his action upon the world. He expresses this immanently experienced self in the symbol of the heart, and by positing that expression comes to a new level of knowledge and volition. This new level is a further act of self-realization. Thus the symbol gathers up and expresses in a unified way what man knows himself to be.[53]

1.1.3.3. *Summary*

Thus far we have seen how Rahner proceeds from an analysis of the use of the word "heart" and the discovery that it is a "primordial word" to an analysis of the ontological basis for symbolism in general and for the symbol of the heart in particular. Since Rahner himself does this explicitly in terms of a *theological* ontology, i.e., applying the truths of Catholic theology to the insights of a general ontology, we have also followed

---

[52] Cf. Rahner, *Geist in Welt, passim.*

[53] The fifth characteristic, corruptibility, is due to the nature of symbolic thought itself. Precisely because it is unthematic and non-discursive it does not have the characteristics, such as definability, of conceptual thought.

his path through a discussion of some theological implications of symbolism. Finally, having arrived at the principles of symbolism, we returned to an analysis of the use of the word "heart" to show the authenticity and functionality of the symbol. To establish criteria we used the descriptive method of how symbols function and applied Rahner's criteria to this description. We have seen how these descriptive criteria help to explicitate Rahner's criteria.

Thus we have seen how Rahner establishes the ontological and anthropological basis for the symbolic use of the heart to express the complex of psychosomatic activities which make up the human personality. Our next step will be to discuss specifically how this symbol is applied when we speak of the Heart of Christ in the devotion to the Sacred Heart.

1.1.3.4. *Critique*

In common parlance, and even in many dictionary definitions, the word symbol is ordinarily understood to refer to some material object or representation. Thus we might expect to find a primary reliance on physical things in a discussion of symbolism. Such material symbols as a statue of Justice, a national flag, or even the sacramental elements used in ritual are by far the most familiar to us. But this overlooks an important fact, namely, that man's primary use of symbols is a *linguistic* usage.

Rahner's methodology always seeks to begin the discussion of a problem at the level of experience. Thus he begins his discussion of symbolism at the point of most common experience, i.e., linguistic usage, rather than representational usage, of symbols. Some have interpreted this as an abrogation of proper symbolism.[54] However, a true understanding of Rahner's theory of knowledge, based as it is in the psychology of St. Thomas, also reveals that even the formulation of the word itself necessarily depends on the concrete reality named by that word. All human knowing relies on the phantasm, which in turn has its foundation in the concrete, material reality. Thus while Rahner speaks of symbolism in mostly verbal terms, there is necessarily implicit in the word itself the fundamental reference to the concrete object named by the word.

---

[54] Since this criticism is made directly in relation to his writings on the Sacred Heart, we will discuss it at more length in that connection. We mention it here because it implies a general criticism of his theory of symbolism.

1.2.0. The Theology of the Devotion to the Heart of Christ According to Rahner

In this second section we will investigate the use of the heart in the Devotion to the Sacred Heart. This will be accomplished in two steps. In the first step we will seek to discover the precise content of the symbol as it is applied to the Lord. In the second step we will look at the Devotion itself in order to see how the symbol of the heart is appropriate to those aspects of the Christian mysteries to which the Devotion seeks to draw attention. We will approach these steps with specific reference to Rahner's writings on the Devotion.

1.2.1.0. The Use of the Heart as Symbol in the Devotion

For Rahner

> Heart ... denotes the core of the human person which is original and inmost with respect to everything else in the human person ... at which therefore man is originally and wholly related to other persons and above all also to God .... [55]

From this we can see that the symbol of the heart involves us in a two-fold movement. The first is a movement inward, in which the "core of the human person" is discovered. The second is a movement outward, in which that personal center which is symbolized in the heart relates to others and to God.

When we apply this symbol to Jesus Christ, we find that the same two-fold movement is involved. In the inward movement we come to the "core" of his person, that unique conjunction of the Divine and human which we call the Hypostatic Union. In the outward movement we come to the unique relationship which Christ has to all men and to the Father, a relationship we call Mediatorship. We will now investigate each of these movements in order to clarify the meaning of the symbol, as Rahner understands it, when it is applied to Jesus Christ.

1.2.1.1. *The Inward Movement: Hypostatic Union* [56]

Whe we speak of the Sacred Heart of Jesus we mean primarily the human, fleshy heart of Jesus of Nazareth. But this

---

[55] Rahner, "Theses," *TI* III, p. 332.
[56] Of the two movements this first one receives little explicit treatment in Rahner. It is simply, for the most part, presupposed.

physical heart, understood in its symbolic meaning, transports
us immediately to the core of his person. It denotes that personal
unity which is uniquely his. As Rahner states it, "... the 'Heart
of Jesus' means the original center of the human reality of the
Son of God ...", "... the original center of our Lord's human
being ...." [57] In this sense we might say that this usage of the
heart as symbol is no different from its usage elsewhere. However, the implications of this usage, precisely because it is the
heart of Jesus Christ of which we are speaking, are infinitely
more profound. For when we speak of the "center of our Lord's
human being," we are transported immediately into the realm of
the mystery of God himself. For that concrete, historical human
nature which was assumed by the Logos has its being in the
personal unity which is Jesus Christ.[58] Therefore the acts and
attitudes which proceed from that personal core which we symbolize by the heart are the acts and attitudes of the Second
Person of the Trinity. They may not be considered something
extrinsic to the Logos, for that would be the same as saying
that the human nature was not really appropriated and made
his own.[59] Thus the personal center symbolized by the Heart
of Christ *is* at one and the same time the revelation of God
himself. For this reason Rahner says that the theology of the
Devotion could be built around the saying of Jesus: "He that
sees me, sees the Father" (Jn 14:9).[60] Christ reveals both in
what he *is* and in his works and teaching the redemptive love
of God for men. The Heart of Christ is the symbol of that
personal, Hypostatic Unity which man comes to know in those
deeds and words. In this way the symbol of the heart takes
on a new meaning, because it becomes the primary symbol of
love itself.

> That the inmost core of personal reality is love and that love
> is in fact the inmost reality, this is experienced by man only
> in coming to know the heart of the Lord. "Behold this heart,
> which has so loved men": this is not an analytical proposi-

[57] Rahner, "The Eternal Significance of the Humanity of Jesus for
Our Relationship with God," *TI* III, p. 46. Hereafter cited as "Eternal
Significance."

[58] Cf. Denzinger-Schönmetzer, *Enchiridion Symbolorum, Definitionum
et Declarationum*, 34th ed. (Freiburg: Herder, 1965), 300, 318. Hereafter
cited as *DS* followed by the paragraph number.

[59] Rahner, "Theology of the Symbol," *TI* IV, p. 238.

[60] *Ibid.*, p. 237.

tion, derived from the concept of heart, but the shattering consequences of the history of salvation.[61]

Thus in this first inward movement man comes to the discovery of the Person of Christ in and through the symbol of his Heart. This is the discovery that in his Person there is united the Divine and the human in which the Father is revealed.[62] The discovery of that unique personal center leads to the second, outward movement in which the meaning of the actions which proceed from that personal center is discovered.

1.2.1.2. *The Outward Movement : Mediation*

The actions which comprise the outward movement have a double goal : God and mankind. We might consider these under two headings — revelation and reparation.

1.2.1.3. *The Outward Movement Toward Mankind : Revelation*

By the actions which proceed from his divine-human personal center which is symbolized by his heart, Jesus Christ reveals to mankind that the Divine Essence is love. Through his preaching and miracles, and above all by his death and resurrection, Jesus shows himself to be the incarnate Son of God. However, this revelation of God's love, that God is love, is not some kind of vague proposition. That love is revealed quite specifically as *incarnate.* Thus it is a love which in its supreme transcendence enters the world and loves the world which it created as a value in itself. This is the profound meaning of the fact that revelation is incarnate in the history of this world. Thus revelation is not the removal of a veil which allows us to gradually recognize God ever more clearly by avoiding or ignoring the world around us. [63]

Furthermore, because that Divine Love is incarnate and reveals itself to us in and through creation and the history of mankind, we can only come into contact with the God who *so* reveals himself by a religious act which passes through the reality of this world which is loved by God in and for itself. [64]

----

[61] Rahner, "Preliminaries," *TI* III, p. 327.

[62] Exactly *what* is discovered in the Person of Christ will be treated in our third chapter where we will attempt to verify the symbol of the Sacred Heart, as Rahner interprets it, in the light of his Christology.

[63] Rahner, "Eternal Meaning," *TI* III, p. 40.

[64] *Ibid.*, p. 41.

Thus God reveals himself to us as love by the very act of loving
his creation, and mankind in particular. This he accomplishes
in a radical and irreversible way by making his own that creaturely, human reality.   In this way, the discovery of the personal center of Jesus Christ which is symbolized by his heart
is the discovery of the incomprehensible love of God for mankind.   Thus Jesus Christ is the mediating means in which God
reveals himself, and mankind discovers him, as love. [65]

1.2.1.4.   *The Outward Movement Toward God: Reparation*

This outward movement from God to mankind which is
revealed in Jesus Christ is accompanied by a second outward
movement of man to God. This is the movement we call reparation or atonement. By the loving actions which proceed from
his personal center, especially by his Passion and Death, Jesus
Christ accomplishes for mankind the forgiveness of sin which
separates man from God. Thus mankind is once again joined
to God in sonship, which is accomplished by the gift of the Holy
Spirit. In this way revelation is not simply the announcement
of a set of truths or facts; rather the actions of Christ are seen
to have a real, existential effect on the state of man. Through
the redemption gained by the Lord, each man is capable of
experiencing the end of the alienation and separation from God
caused by sin and can appropriate as his own the experience
of being loved by God. This, too, is accomplished by the mediation of Christ.

> Jesus Christ is the mediator. He is that unity in which God ...
> has assumed the multiplicity of reality ... He did this when he
> assumed creaturehood ... in the mode of a spiritual being. In
> assuming it he made it his own reality, which remains eternally
> his own (even in its multiplicity), and yet it is precisely in
> virtue of this fact that this reality of creaturehood ... is re-
> deemed, set free for and drawn abidingly into the indivisible
> unity of God.[66]

1.2.1.5.   *Summary*:

From this brief treatment we can see that all the essential
elements of a Christology are present in the symbol of the Heart

---

[65] *Ibid.*, p. 43.
[66] Rahner, "Theological Meaning," *TI* VIII, p. 218.

of Christ. [67]   There are two points here which should be emphasized before we go on to speak of the devotion itself.   The
first is that incarnation remains the permanent condition of
Christ.   Thus devotion to the Heart of Christ cannot simply
be a backward looking devotion which concerns itself solely
with past actions which proceeded from that personal center
which is symbolized by the heart.   Rather the devotion must
seek to existentially realize that even now, in its "glorified state,"
the humanity of Jesus is still active in the ongoing work of the
salvation of mankind.   The human heart of Christ perdures to
all eternity and thus provides us with the true meaning of honor-
ing that heart in a cultic way in the here and now. [68]

The second point which must be emphasized is actually
raised as a question: Must every religious act, in order to reach
its final destiny which is God, pass through (implicitly, at least)
the humanity of Christ? [69]   Rahner says that theology has not
yet worked out the presuppositions of such a claim to allow it
to be made in a definitive way.   It seems, however, that Rahner
himself tends toward this position.   He says that "there can
and should be such a theology." [70]   And this position is certainly
consistent with his radically incarnational understanding of
Christian existence.   If this presupposition is true, it bears
directly on the question of the Sacred Heart.   "If the 'Heart of
Jesus' means the original centre of the human reality of the
Son of God, then there must be a basic religious act which is
mediated by and goes through this centre to God." [71]

We shall now proceed to our second point, dealing specifically with the devotion and its forms.   In so doing we will see
how these two points play a role in the devotion itself.

1.2.2.0.   THE FORM OF THE DEVOTION AND ITS RELATIONSHIP TO THE SYMBOL

In this section we shall present Rahner's thought on the
concrete form of the Devotion to the Sacred Heart.   In doing
so we shall emphasize the theological background and content
of the various practices associated with the devotion.   We shall

---

[67] This will be verified in our second chapter on Rahner's Christology.
[68] Rahner, "Eternal Significance," *TI* III, p. 44.
[69] *Ibid.*, p. 44.
[70] *Ibid.*, p. 46.
[71] *Ibid.*, p. 46.

do this under the following headings: historical roots, present relevance, unity of object, multiplicity of forms, reparation, consoling the Lord. Finally we shall deal with the question of the appropriateness and necessity of the symbol in such a devotion.

1.2.2.1. *The Historical Roots of the Devotion* [72]

For Rahner an examination of the historical roots of the Devotion includes not only a return to the sources of the visions of St. Margaret Mary Alacoque at Paray-le-Monial, but also a return to the scriptural, patristic and medieval sources. In this way the dogmatic foundation of the Devotion can be developed. However, this must be done with an explicit realization. The form of the Devotion which has been publicly accepted and promulgated by the Church is that form which developed as a result of the Paray visions. This form is the result of private revelations judged worthy of acceptance by the Church because they met some historically conditioned set of circumstances in the Church. Thus there is a certain contingency to this particular form of the Devotion. The same is not true of its theological foundation, however. For in returning to Scripture and tradition one is able to formulate more precisely what the object of the Devotion is and what forms of honor are appropriate to the Devotion. In so doing we move out of the area of historical contingency and into the area of the permanency of the essential elements of the Christian life. [73] This kind of process would

---

[72] Here we must mention a fundamental conflict which arises in the historical interpretation of the sources of the Devotion. The conflict deals with the evaluation of the whole patristic tradition of the exegesis of John 7:37-41 (the saying on "streams of living water shall flow from his bosom") and of John 19:34 (the piercing of the side of Christ with the soldier's lance). One school, represented by A. Hamon (cf. *Histoire de la Dévotion au Sacré-Coeur*, v. II: *L'Aube de la Dévotion*, Paris, 1925) and K. Richstätter, *Das Herz des Welterlösers* (Freiburg: Herder, 1932), would argue for a certain discontinuity between the patristic and medieval periods. The other school, represented by Hugo Rahner and J. Stierli (cf. *Heart of the Savior*, New York, 1958) would argue for considerable continuity between the two eras, especially as witnessed in the exegetical continuity between the patristic era and the early Middle Ages in their interpretation of these texts. Karl Rahner would definitely share the viewpoint of his brother Hugo and Stierli (cf. K. Rahner, " 'Coeur de Jesus' chez Origène?" *RAM* 14 (1934), 171-174). This question is important because it directly affects the respective viewpoints as to the breadth of interpretation of the Devotion itself. We will see this in the course of our discussion.

[73] Rahner, "Theses," *TI* III, p. 337f.

be essential to enable contemporary movements aimed at reviving the Devotion to the Sacred Heart to be fruitful and effective.

This position of Rahner's about how far back into the past one can trace the Devotion and the consequences one can draw for the contemporary situation of the Devotion will have its conclusions illustrated when we speak of the object and the forms of the Devotion. This historical perspective is fundamental for understanding why Rahner holds the positions he does, and the lack of this perspective or the rejection of it is the basis for much of the criticism which is levelled against Rahner.

1.2.2.2. *Contemporary Relevance of the Devotion*

A knowledge of the history of the Devotion produces an understanding of the situation in which the Devotion found such popular acceptance and at the same time gives us a perspective of how the Devotion can be effective today. For Rahner the situation in which the Devotion found such acceptance was *not* the era of St. Margaret Mary (17th century), nor the era of Jansenism (18th century), but rather "the situation of modern times in general (which first made its appearance with the French Revolution)." [74] Rahner characterizes this situation as the age of industrialization and secularization, an age wherein the external supports of a specifically Christian viewpoint have been removed, an age wherein "... the Christian religion ... becomes more plainly dependent upon the inner, most personal decision of faith of the individual ...." [75] The world proclaims the absence of God and the Christian finds himself existentially reliving the experience of the "... Jesus of Gethsemane and Golgotha ...." [76]

It is against this background that the Devotion, with its emphasis on interiority, the discovery of the love of God, and reparation for the failure of men to return that love, finds the historical conditions which account for its popular acceptance by the whole Church. Since this is still our contemporary situation, the Devotion maintains its ability to attract the attention of Christians everywhere. [77] However, Rahner insists that it would be a mistake to absolutize past forms and perspectives

---

[74] *Ibid.*, p. 339.
[75] *Ibid.*, p. 339.
[76] *Ibid.*, p. 340.
[77] *Ibid.*, p. 341. Cf. Hugo Rahner, "Mirabilis Progressio: Gedanken zur Geschichtstheologie der Herz-Jesu-Verehrung," *Cor Jesu* I, ed. Bea, et al., (Rome: Herder, 1969), pp. 23-58.

of the Devotion. Its past shortcomings must be addressed and corrected to bring it into line with the situation today. This involves working out its Trinitarian context, and as a corollary to this, placing emphasis on the *mediatorship* of Christ in such a way that we pass through, with and in the mediation of his Heart, to the Father. [78]

When we look at the contemporary situation we find that not much has changed in three hundred years. Many of the initial causes of the Church's restraint to approve the Devotion are still with us. It has generally been accepted that *latria* can be offered to the individual parts of the humanity of Christ. But there is no clear agreement on the precise object of the Devotion, and the Devotion itself suffers at the hands of those who would make exaggerated claims on its behalf as well as at the hands of those who would downplay it because its external manifestations have made them have a negative judgment even about the essential elements of the Devotion. [79]

---

[78] *Ibid.*, p. 340f.

[79] Cf. Richard Gutzwiller, "The Opposition," *Heart of the Saviour, op. cit.*, pp. 1-14; and H. Rahner, "Mirabilis Progressio", *Cor Jesu* I, pp. 23-58. In many ways the liturgical history of the Feast of the Sacred Heart is a paradigm of the shifting attitudes in the Church regarding the Devotion. Between 1668 and 1929 we find eight approved Mass texts and four strictly local texts. There are differences of accent in each of them. Furthermore, it was not until 1856 that Pius IX promulgated the celebration of the Feast for the Church Universal. In 1889 Leo XIII raised the Feast to a double of the first class, and in 1929 Pius XI, in promulgating the text *Cogitationes* further enhanced the Feast with an octave. The octave was dropped by Pius XII in the liturgical reforms of 1955. Some might interpret the encyclical letter *Haurietis Aquas* of Pius XII in 1956 as the final word on the Devotion. However, further development of accents and continued opposition are evident in the reform of the liturgy after Vatican II. For example, two new sets of readings for Year A and Year C of the lectionary cycle show the emphasis placed on covenant love (Year A) and the Shepherd of Israel-Good Shepherd theme (Year C). Year B retains the emphasis on the revelation of God's love in Christ which was the theme of the Mass *Cogitationes*. The Entrance and Communion Verses from *Cogitationes* have been retained, along with the Collect, which emphasizes reparation, from that Mass. The second Collect in the new *Missale Romanum* is essentially taken from the Mass *Miserebitur*, approved on January 2, 1765, by the Congregation of Rites for Poland, Spain and the Archconfraternity of the Sacred Heart in Rome. This Collect emphasizes the love of Christ as the model for the love of Christians. Cf. A. Bugnini, "Le Messe del Ss. Cuore di Gesù," *Cor Jesu* I, pp. 61-94, for a comparison of the pre-Vatican II Mass texts. Continued opposition to the Feast is insinuated by A. Olivar in the reform of the Roman Calendar. This fluctuating liturgical history "... basta da

1.2.2.3. *The Unity of Object of the Devotion*

> Let us ... face the fact that theologians do not agree upon what
> is the object of this devotion. Some hold it is the earthly,
> bodily Heart of our Lord ... others maintain that the proper
> object of the cult is the love of Christ .... The third school of
> opinion makes the physical human heart of our Lord the ob-
> ject of the cult, but sees this heart as the symbol of love ... the
> heart is the material, Christ's love the formal object of the
> cult. This position is almost reversed by the fourth school,
> which maintains that love is the material object, and its sym-
> bolization in the heart the formal object. Finally a fifth school
> would find the material object in the "Cor Ethicum," and the
> formal object in the relation of this "Cor Ethicum" to the plan
> of Redemption.[80]

This citation amply documents the difficulties we face when
we speak of the object of the Devotion to the Sacred Heart.
It is precisely in this area that Rahner has tried to make an
original contribution. We will first deal with the problems con-
nected with each of these positions and then present Rahner's
position.

1) *Bodily Heart*

This position rightly sees the basis of the Devotion in the
truth of the Hypostatic Union. It is because of this union that
Christ's humanity is worthy of *latria*. However, with no symbolic understanding this position cannot answer the question
of what is so special about the heart, and why precisely this
part, and not another, of Christ's humanity is so specially singled
out for worship. [81]

---

sola a dimostrare la fluttuazione dottrinale che ha accompagnato tale
festa per il fatto che è difficile da definire — e anche da giustificare —
dal punto di vista liturgico. Recentemente non sono mancati tentativi
di spiegare la solennità alla luce del Mistero pasquale; qualcuno anzi ha
proposto di celebrare semplicemente l'amore del Cuore di Gesù al Venerdì
Santo." A. Olivar, *Il nuovo calendario liturgico* (Torino: LDC, 1973),
p. 205f. Nevertheless, the Feast of the Sacred Heart has retained its
liturgical status and is celebrated as a Solemnity. P. Pierre Jounel,
Chairman of the *Coetus de calendario* of the *Consilium ad exsequendam
Constitutionem de Sacra Liturgia*, in a letter dated January 20, 1976, says
that opposition to retaining the feast was expressed by only one member
of the *Coetus*.

[80] R. Gutzwiller, "The Opposition," in Stierli, *op. cit.*, p. 5.

[81] For a shallow and somewhat offensive evaluation of the Devotion
which is based on this understanding, cf. Firth, *op. cit.*, pp. 411-414.

2) *Love of Christ*

This position stresses one of the main aspects of the content of the Devotion, but loses the connection with the symbol. In effect this position does away with the need for the symbol, and cannot answer the question of why we would even need a special Devotion to the love of Christ when we have direct access to it through the Holy Spirit.

3) *Third and Fourth Opinions*

These positions, although directly opposed, try to stress the connection between the symbol and its content. In effect, however, the symbol is somewhat extrinsic in these opinions and functions more on the level of a sign.

4) *"Cor Ethicum"*

This position, which is more typical of modern thought on the Devotion, affords a richness of interpretation which is the direct result of scholarly research into the scriptural and traditional sources of the Devotion. But here again the symbol of the heart does not have an intrinsic role to play in the Devotion itself. It lacks any real mediating function.

5) *Rahner's Position*

It is against the background of these difficulties that Rahner has attempted to work out his solution to the problem of the object of the Devotion. In effect we can say that he has attempted to provide a real place in the Devotion for the physical heart of the Lord and, at the same time, to provide the possibility of allowing that physical heart to be capable of the richness of interpretation of the "Cor Ethicum" position.

We can say that the "Cor Ethicum" position is typical of the Innsbruck theologians. Heinrich Noldin posthumously published Lempl's manuscript *Das Herz Jesu: Eine Studie über die verschiedenen Bedeutungen des Wortes "Herz" und über den Gegenstand der kirchlichen Herz-Jesu-Andacht* in 1909, and beginning in 1914, with the publication of the tenth edition of his own work, *Die Andacht zum heiligsten Herzen Jesu*, he himself adopts the position of the "Cor Ethicum." [82]

---

[82] Cf. R. Tucci, "Storia della letteratura relativa al culto del S. Cuore di Gesù," *Cor Jesu* II, pp. 582-584. In Footnotes 267-270 on these pages, Tucci mentions Jungmann, Müller, Lercher, Dander and K. Rahner all

We can also say that Rahner himself represented this same position, with, in Tucci's judgment, "personal developments," [83] until the publication of his article "Zur Theologie des Symbols" in 1959.[84] Until that time Rahner's position could be considered a classical expression of the "Cor Ethicum" position. Thus the use of the heart in the Devotion connotes "the self-same total-human primordial word 'heart' as the inmost original core of the body-soul totality of the person." [85]   Thus the material object of the Devotion is "the Lord with respect to this his heart." [86] The formal object of the Devotion would be this love as exhibited in his redemptive acts "which gives form and unity to his relationships to us." [87]   This position of Rahner's, although proposed as "theses," i.e., in a provisorial way, leaves the role of the physical heart in the Devotion unclear, precisely because the concept of symbolism is undeveloped.[88]

We can say that this critique of Rahner's position was practically universal. Thus, for example, the critique of J.-A. Robillard: "The intention is good: to battle against the present disaffection by discarding all sweet sentimentality, but the realisation is a good deal worse, which consists in putting the heart of flesh of our Lord as far as possible in the background." [89]

Since the publication of "Zur Theologie des Symbols," there can be no doubt about the place which Rahner gives to the physical heart of the Lord in the Devotion. The physical heart of the Lord is the object of the Devotion because as the real

---

as representatives of this position. It seems that the biblical and historical research of H. Rahner is aimed at securing the foundations of this position.

[83] *Ibid.*, p. 584, note 270.

[84] Cf. *Cor Jesu* I, pp. 463-505, and *TI* IV, pp. 221-252.

[85] Rahner, "Theses," *TI* III, p. 343f.

[86] *Ibid.*, p. 344.

[87] *Ibid.*, p. 344.

[88] Cf. Tucci, *Cor Jesu* II, p. 622.

[89] J.A. Robillard, Review of *Le Coeur du Sauveur*, Fr. translation of *Cor Salvatoris* (ed. J. Stierli), in *La Vie Spirituelle* 95 (1956), 209f. Orig.: "L'intention est bonne: lutter contre la désaffection actuelle en écartant toute sentimentalité doucereuse, mais la réalisation l'est beaucoup moins, qui consiste à mettre le plus en retrait qu'il est possible le coeur de chair du Seigneur."   Concurring opinions in other reviews of *Cor Salvatoris*, cf. C. Geffré in *RSPT* 41 (1957), 544-547; Tucci in *La Civiltà Cattolica* (1957), I, 182-194; M. Donnelly in *TS* 18 (1967), 288-289; cf. also J. Galot, "Quel est l'objet de la devotion au Sacré-Coeur, *NRT* 77 (1955), 924-938; J. Sweeney, "Recent Developments in Dogmatic Theology," *TS* 17 (1956), 368-413, especially 388-405.

symbol of the person and redemptive meaning of Christ it is both posited by these and makes them really be there, be present, for all men. Furthermore, this understanding of the heart as real symbol allows Rahner to insist upon the radical unity of the object of the Devotion. No longer is it necessary to make a distinction between the material and formal objects of the Devotion. Precisely because the heart functions as a symbol in the sense in which Rahner has developed that term it unites the two terms of the distinction as it mediates them to us. Thus the heart points to the more original unity of the whole in the person of Christ.

> It [heart] is used as a "primordial word" of religious speech, and signifies from the start the unity of both [i.e., physical heart and inwardness of Christ] — a unity which has not to be created subsequently, as when an object is linked to a sign exterior to it as its symbolic representation. The unity is more original than the distinction, because the symbol is a distinct and yet intrinsic moment of the reality as it manifests itself.[90]

This position of Rahner's helps us to unite certain perspectives of the Devotion. For example, it enables us to speak, as *Haurietis Aquas* does, of the "threefold love" of Christ and at the same time to see the unity of that love in the person of Christ. Thus the divine, Trinitarian love which the Word shares with the Father and the Spirit, the infused charity of Christ's human soul and the natural "emotional affection" of his human nature all find their proper symbol in his Heart precisely because the heart is the natural, primordial symbol of that prior unity of the Person of Christ in which that divine-human love finds its incarnate expression.[91]

Furthermore, it enables us to unite the symbol and the symbolized in such a way that their formal prior unity is perceived as an intrinsic relationship. In this way the place of the heart in the Devotion is secured because it is perceived as the necessary mediating means for arriving at that consoling and atoning love of Christ which is the major concern of the Devotion. Only if this intrinsic relationship is perceived can we avoid what

---

[90] Rahner, "The Theology of the Symbol," *TI* IV, pp. 251f. Brackets mine. Cf. Tucci's comment that Rahner's clarification of symbolism in this article "dissipates any doubt" about the role of the physical heart in the Devotion: Tucci, *Cor Jesu* II, p. 622, note 421.

[91] *AAS* 48 (1956), 327f.

Rahner calls the "fatal question" [92] of why we need to bother with the symbol of the bodily Heart of Christ.

> Reality and its appearance in the flesh are precisely in Christianity forever one, unmixed and indivisible. The reality of the divine self-revelation creates for itself its divine immediacy inasmuch as it makes itself present in the symbol; this symbol does not mediate by dividing, but unites immediately, because the true symbol is united to the symbolised inasmuch as the symbolised posits the symbol as its own self-realization.[93]

1.2.2.4. *The Multilpicity of Forms of the Devotion*

While insisting on the radical unity of the object of the Devotion, Rahner argues for allowing a multiplicity of forms of the Devotion. He does this on two grounds: first, the historical interpretation of the Devotion, and second, general ascetical principles. First, a proper historical perspective helps us to understand that there is a difference "between the practice of the devotion and its subsequent reflexive description." [94] Thus the history of the Devotion is written as a reflection upon that which is practiced, and there remains the question of whether the subsequent reflection has done justice to what is experienced in the practice of the Devotion. Therefore we must admit that theological and historical reflection upon devotional practice often does not capture the real depth of what is experienced. Historically we can say that the Devotion has taken many forms: "that of the mystic, that of the person deeply moved by his redemption, that of the genuine piety of the 'average' Christian, that of creative originality, that ... in accord with traditional

---

[92] Rahner, "The Theology of the Symbol," *TI* IV, p. 252.

[93] Translation mine. German text: Wirklichkeit und ihre Erscheinung im Fleisch sind eben im Christentum unvermischt und untrennbar für immer eins. Die Wirklichkeit der göttlichen Selbstmitteilung shafft sich gerade dadurch ihre göttliche Unmittelbarkeit, dass sie sich im Symbol gegenwärtig setzt, das nicht trennend vermittelt, sondern unmittelbar eint, weil das eigentliche Symbol mit dem Symbolisierten dadurch real geeint ist, dass dieses jenes als seinen eigenen Selbstvollzug setzt." *Schriften* IV, p. 311. Text from *Theological Investigations*: "Reality and its appearance in the flesh are forever one in Christianity, inconfused and inseparable. The reality of the divine self-communication creates for itself its immediacy by constituting itself present in the symbol, which does not divide as it mediates but unites immediately, because the true symbol is united with the thing symbolized, since the latter constitutes the former as its own self-realization." *TI* IV, p. 252.

[94] Rahner, "Theses," *TI* III, p. 334.

norms ...." [95]   Here we would even have to include those expressions of the Devotion which might be considered a deviation.[96] Any attempt to encompass all of these under the mode of only one of them would inevitably lead to distortion. Thus while the Paray-le-Monial mode of the Devotion is a cardinal point in the history of the Devotion and is the means by which the Devotion achieved approval by the Church and found its liturgical expression, we must nevertheless admit that there are other forms of the Devotion.

Rahner's second reason for arguing for a multiplicity of forms of the Devotion is based on general principles of the spiritual life. First of all, devotion to the Sacred Heart has a special place in the spectrum of Christian devotions. It is not simply something on the same level as devotion to the saints, or even devotion to Mary. Nevertheless, devotion to the Sacred Heart is not simply the same as Christianity either. Therefore the introduction of the Devotion into the spiritual life of Christians is a matter of discernment.[97] Thus the question of what role, if any, this Devotion is to play in the life of the individual Christian, as well as the question of which practices and forms of the Devotion are proper to the individual's stage of development, are matter for discernment, i.e., essentially of allowing grace the freedom to guide the individual.[98]

We can state what Rahner is saying in another way. The forms which this or any devotion takes serve a functional purpose with regard to achieving the end of the devotion. Primacy belongs to achieving that end. The Heart of Christ is presented to us for our devotion because it is a powerful symbol which leads us directly to the fulness of Christ. In and through this symbol, the fulness of his Person and the meaning of his saving actions are made present to us. They disclose themselves to be Love, pure and simple. They further elicit acts of responsive love on our part, acts of loving adoration of God in and through Christ, and acts of loving service of mankind as the proper moral response to what the symbol discloses. The Church has approved certain forms of devotional response which are fitting for this devotion. But this cannot be interpreted in a narrow sense, so that only where these specific devotional acts are found is there

---

[95] *Ibid.*, p. 334.
[96] *Ibid.*, p. 334.
[97] *Ibid.*, pp. 342f.
[98] *Ibid.*, p. 343.

true devotion to the Sacred Heart. Rather, each individual remains free to follow the guidance of the Spirit and to form responses which are expressions of the depths of spiritual insight
with which he has been graced as a result of his knowing and
loving encounter with the Heart of the Lord.

1.2.2.5. *Reparation*

One of the main aspects of the Paray mode of the Devotion to the Sacred Heart is the prayer and practice of reparation made to Christ to atone for the rejection of the love which
is revealed in his Heart. Rahner seeks to give this practice a
theological interpretation and to accent certain pastoral, peda-
gogical principles for this practice.

Theologically, Rahner sees the practice of reparation as a
constitutive element in the loving response to the love of Christ
which is revealed in the symbol. The discovery of that love in
the symbol of the Heart creates a response which involves a
"sharing in the accomplishment of this redemptive love and in
its fate in the world: reparation." [99] The essence of reparation
is to be found in the Christian's being conformed in grace to
Christ, a conformity which necessarily involves the "... loving
acceptance of a share in the fate of the Lord ...." [100] Prayers and
deeds in which this reparation finds its expression are "preliminary exercises" for that complete and total conformity to
Christ which every Christian must undergo in facing his own
death.[101] Thus reparation, because it takes place, as does the
whole Christian life, "in Christ Jesus," has an expiatory character
regardless of the presence or absence of an explicit, conscious
intention. This is an important point to bear in mind when
dealing with the question of how much expiation should be in-
troduced into a person's spiritual life.[102]

Again Rahner introduces the Trinitarian structure of salvation to suggest certain principles for the prayer and preaching
of reparation. There is nothing objectionable in addressing
prayers of reparation to Christ, since his redemptive work of
expiation is also addressed to himself as the Second Person of

---

[99] *Ibid.*, p. 344f.
[100] *Ibid.*, p. 345.
[101] *Ibid.*, p. 345. Cf. Rahner, "The Passion and Asceticism," *TI* III,
p. 58ff., esp. 74-82, and *ibid.*, "On the Theology of Death," *Quaestiones
Disputatae* 2 (New York: Herder and Herder, 1961), esp. pp. 56-80.
[102] *Ibid.*, p. 345.

the Trinity. But since the general movement of Christian life is in the Spirit, with Christ, to the Father, Rahner suggests that it would be more desirable to emphasize the mediating role of Christ in prayers and preaching about the theme of reparation, as well as to emphasize that our works of reparation are a participation in and carrying on of his work of reparation, in and through the Church.[103]

1.2.2.6. Consoling the Lord

Another practice of the Devotion which Rahner has addressed is the contemplation of the Passion of Christ during the "Holy Hour," a practice known as consoling the Lord. Rahner again seeks to give a theological interpretation to this practice as well as draw some conclusions for pastoral pedagogy. Theologically, it is not very desirable that in this contemplation of the Passion, which concentrates on past historical events and makes them present as if the time span of two thousand years did not exist, the present glorified state of Christ should be lost from view. Thus we do not console the Lord by "pretending" that those historical events are being re-enacted and by making ourselves participants in a kind of imaginary passion play. Nor can we ignore those historical events and concentrate only on the glory of Christ. Rather, Rahner says we must address our prayers of consolation to the glorified Christ who in his glory still bears the marks of his suffering. Thus the contemplation of the Passion must include the notion that it was in and through this suffering and death that Christ became the glorified Lord.[104]

Traditional theology has justified this practice by referring to the infused knowledge of Christ. Thus Christ "foreknew" all the good deeds of all men of all ages, and this knowledge consoled him in the sufferings of his Passion. Rahner, however, says that this position is not at all self-evident, and therefore it "could be asked whether the inconceivably dreadful and boundless depth of his inner suffering at the God-forsakenness of this sinful world" [105] was not so total as to exclude the consoling effect that any such foreknowledge might have had.

Rahner then goes on to say that if anything did actually console the Lord, it would have been the daily living out of

---

[103] *Ibid.*, p. 346f.
[104] *Ibid.*, p. 347f.
[105] *Ibid.*, p. 349.

Christian existence in the power of the grace which Christ won
for us through his Passion, and this independent of any specific
intention or conscious practice of consoling the Lord.[106]   Thus
Rahner concludes that this practice is not essential to the Devotion and should not be preached as such.[107]

What then is the sense of the Holy Hour and the contemplation of the Passion? According to Rahner it is the contemplation of the Lord who through his suffering has become the
glorified One. In this consideration the Christian contemplates
and appropriates the "law" of faith and obedience which has
been planted in his own heart by the grace of Christ. By the
power of this grace his life is conformed to Christ's, so that
faithful obedience to the Will of the Father becomes in ever-
increasing measure the goal of his existence.[108]

> By these what is of importance is already in point of fact
> given in a simple way: that the head of the Church, even in
> the earthly life, participated in all that has happened and will
> happen throughout the whole of history in all the members of
> his Body as in mourning so also in consolation.[109]

1.2.2.7. *The Necessity of the Symbol of the Heart of Jesus*

We have seen that the Devotion to the Sacred Heart com-
bines many essential elements of Christian life: the existential
discovery of the meaning of the Person and words of Jesus Christ;
the appropriation and practice of the essential dynamism of
grace, i. e., becoming conformed to Christ; the mandate to return
the love of God revealed in Christ by our own works of love;
reparation for our own sins and the sinfulness of the world.
The question can be raised, and has been, whether one needs
such a devotion in order to achieve these goals.[110]

Rahner answers this question of necessity on two levels.
One cannot claim an absolute necessity for thi Devotion. It is
not simply the same as Christianity itself, and any attempts to

---

[106] *Ibid.*, p. 349.

[107] *Ibid.*, p. 350.

[108] *Ibid.*, pp. 348 and 351.

[109] *Ibid.*, p. 351. It is interesting to note that many of those who
criticized Rahner for his "Theses" (cf. *supra*, note 89), nevertheless expressed approval of his theological and pastoral interpretation of the
practices of reparation and consoling the Lord.

[110] Cf. J. Galot, *op. cit.*, NRT 77 (1955), 924-938; I. N. Zorè, "Recentiorum quaestionum de cultu Ss. Cordis Jesu conspectus: (utrum crisis an
evolutio cultus praevideatur?), *Gregorianum* 37 (1956), 104-120.

make it such are misguided. Furthermore, many Christians can and do achieve the same goals as the Devotion proposes without any explicit devotion to the Heart of Christ as such. Again, the Devotion as we know it did not always exist, whereas the constitutive elements of the Christian life have always been present in the Church.[111]

On another level, however, Rahner does speak of a kind of necessity, if not of this particular Devotion, then at least of the use of a unifying symbol capable of epitomizing these and other essential elements of the Christian life. Unity and multiplicity are the ontological condition of being. They are therefore two of the dynamic existentials of human existence. Man can possess himself in unity only by becoming fragmented in the multiplicity of the world. And while going out of himself into that multiplicity he experiences the necessity of seeking to reunite everything in one. This existential dynamism applies *a fortiori* to his religious experience. Man can never fully possess in unity the abundant fulness of God. If he is to seek it, he must seek it in Christ who at one and the same time is both the fulness of God and the fulness of man. This is the only "place" where this unity is available to him. At the same time he needs some kind of unifying formula or symbol in order to reach the fulness of the abundant mystery of Christ.

In this sense Rahner would argue for the necessity of a symbol in order to achieve this unity. There is no necessity that the symbol used be the heart. In fact, Rahner argues that such words as "logos" were symbols for the men of their times. However, he insists that in the present context we have no other word or symbol which is capable of capturing and expressing in one the dynamic multiplicity and fulness of the mystery of Christ, no other word or symbol except this one, heart.[112]

> Here we have, united and reconciled at their source, all the realities of the Father's incarnate Word and therefore all the immense variety of experience which we go through with him. When we say "Sacred Heart of Jesus" we evoke that primally unifying center, at once incomprehensible and perfectly matter-of-fact, which displays itself at work in the history of Jesus of Nazareth, which alone gives meaning to this history and its

---

[111] Cf. Rahner, "Theological Meaning," *TI* VIII, p. 219, and *idem.*, "Unity-Love-Mystery," *TI* VIII, p. 229.

[112] *Ibid.*, pp. 220-223. If it is true that the Devotion is on the decline today, it is also true that no new symbol has been found to replace it.

every event, the meaning of God, his incomprehensibility, his love, the meaning of life that finds itself through death.[113]

Man *must* seek the "unifying center" of his religious experience. He *can* find it in the Heart of Christ.

1.2.3.0. CONCLUSION TO CHAPTER I

In this chapter we have followed Rahner's thought on the Devotion to the Sacred Heart, beginning with his ontology of symbolism and ending with his application of that understanding of symbolism to the use of the symbol of the heart in the Devotion. This has produced certain clarifications about the content of the Devotion. These clarifications fulfill the task established by the first part of Rahner's first principle of symbolism.[114]

The second part of that task, namely, the relationship of that particular symbolization of Christ to the totality of Christology will be the topic of our third chapter. Before we can draw out that relationship, however, it is necessary to present a synthesis of Rahner's Christology. In light of that synthesis, then, we will be able to isolate those elements of Rahner's theology of the Devotion to the Sacred Heart which have a direct relationship to the symbol of the Heart of Jesus which is the object of that Devotion.

---

[113] Rahner, "The Man with the Pierced Heart," *Servants of the Lord* (New York: Herder and Herder, 1968), p. 116.

[114] Cf. *supra*, p. 33.

CHAPTER II

CHRISTOLOGICAL THEMES IN THE WRITINGS OF KARL RAHNER

2.0. INTRODUCTION

The purpose of this chapter is to give a general overview of Rahner's Christology. We have purposely used the word "themes" in the chapter title because it is not our intention to present an exhaustive, detailed study of the material. That work has already been done elsewhere,[1] and would not only take us far afield but also make us lose sight of the reason for including a chapter of this kind: to verify the content of the symbol of the Heart of Christ in terms of its theoretical-systematic presentation in Christology. In our first chapter we saw that the symbol of the Heart of Christ presents us with a two-fold movement: an inward movement toward Christ's personal center in which the reality we call Hypostatic Union is discovered; and an outward movement toward God and man in which reparation and revelation as realities mediated in and through Christ are discovered, in other words, Christ's mediatorship.[2] In this chapter we propose to study these two themes in Rahner's Christology to determine more precisely what we are presented with when the symbol of the Heart of Christ involves us in this movement.

2.1.0. THE PERSON OF CHRIST: HYPOSTATIC UNION

Rahner's Christology, as his theology in general, is based on the transcendental metaphysics of Neo-Scholasticism. This

---

[1] Cf. B. van den Heijden, *Karl Rahner: Darstellung und Kritik seiner Grundposition* (Einsiedeln: Johannes Verlag, 1973); H. Geiber, "Die Interpretation der kirchlichen Lehre vom Gottmenschen bei Karl Rahner, S.J.," *Kerygma und Dogma* 14 (1968) 307-330; W. Kasper, "Christologie von Unten?" *Grundfragen der Christologie heute, Quaestiones Disputatae* 72, ed. L. Scheffczyk (Freiburg: Herder, 1975), pp. 153ff.

[2] Cf. *supra*, p. 46ff.

metaphysical Christology represents one of the two basic types of Christology. The other type is what Rahner calls the *heilsge-schichtlicher* type.[3] The basic starting point of a metaphysical Christology is the *"verbum caro factum est"* of Jn 1:14.[4] This type of Christology can basically be described as Christology "from above," a Christology which takes such concepts as the pre-existence of the Word, his divinity and his distinction from the Father as postulates based on certain sayings of Jesus in the Gospels, and proceeds from these to a metaphysical discussion of the relationship between the divine and the human in Christ, and the cosmic and transcendental meaning of the Incarnation.[5] The starting point emphasizes the divinity of Christ with the result that, throughout a Christology of this type, this emphasis remains. Rahner, while clearly a member of this camp, has seen in this starting point and emphasis the possibility of distortion, at least in the existential appreciation of the mystery of the Hypostatic Union, and as a result has tried to avoid those distortions in his own writings.[6] We shall discuss these distortions as problems in the horizon of understanding and Rahner's attempts to avoid them in his own writings on the Hypostatic Union.

2.1.1. THE ABSOLUTE UNITY OF CHRIST

Rahner's starting point for discussing the unity of the divine and human natures in the one person of Christ is the definition of the Council of Chalcedon.[7] The Council's dialectical definition of the union of the two natures in Christ as being "unconfused, unchangeable, undivided and inseparable" is both the

---

[3] Rahner, "Die zwei Grundtypen der Christologie," *Schriften* X, p. 227. *ET* in *TI* VIII, pp. 213-223. *Heilsgeschichtlicher* means a Christology which concentrates on the events of the life of Jesus as events of saving history.

[4] *Ibid.*, p. 232 and *idem*, "On the Theology of the Incarnation," *TI* IV, p. 105.

[5] *Ibid.*, p. 231f.

[6] As we shall see, Rahner has achieved this by reference to the realities of the life and death of Jesus. It is interesting to note that these realities are precisely the starting point of the other type of Christology and Rahner insists that from a formal methodological point of view even a metaphysical Christology has "its starting point and the possibility of its verification in the first (i.e., *heilsgeschichtlicher*) basic type of Christology." *Ibid.*, p. 231.

[7] Cf. *DS*, 301, 302.

starting point and the hermeneutical principle for judging the adequacy of the results of any Christology. Rahner insists that one cannot do justice to the full actuality of the divine and the human natures in Christ if one conceives of their relationship only in static, ontic terms. Most Christologies arrive at an orthodox, adequate determination of the relationship in these ontic terms, but unless Christology is capable of developing the relationship *also* in ontological-existential terms in which the full dialectic of the Chalcedonian formula can function dynamically, there arises an inevitable problem of the proper understanding of the relationship when it comes to the full and proper functioning of the humanity of Christ.[8]

2.1.2.0. THE HORIZON: PROBLEMS OF UNDERSTANDING

The basic problem we are faced with, then, is how to understand the relationship between the two natures and the one person of Christ in such a way that both the divine and the human are taken seriously, each nature functioning according to its essence, yet both joined into the one person. This is the basic problem on the horizon of understanding Christ, and it arises from different sources.

2.1.2.1. *Methodological Sources of the Problem*

The basic methodological problem arises from the relationship between dogmatic theology and fundamental and biblical theology. Dogmatic theology of a metaphysical type has in general presumed that the questions of the earthly life of Jesus, of his resurrection and of his self-consciousness as evidenced in his witness about himself have all been covered in an adequate way in a fundamental theology. It has considered itself free to involve itself in metaphysical speculation about the person of Christ in a way which abstracted from the problems of fundamental theology. When it finished its speculation it usually failed to reflect on the work it had done and to ask if everything which fundamental theology was concerned with had been adequately dealt with in a speculative way.

In the meanwhile, another problem arises from the work of exegesis and biblical theology. Modern biblical exegesis, using an historical-critical method, has developed a whole area of data

---

[8] K. Rahner, "Current Problems in Christology," *TI* I, pp. 166-173.

dealing with such questions as the knowledge and self-consciousness of the human nature of Christ which cause immediate problems for the systematic theologian. Traditionally, Christology
taught that Christ's human soul was gifted with infused knowledge of all past, present and future events and that he enjoyed
the beatific vision from the first moment of his conception. These
metaphysically deduced statements hardly seem compatible with
the New Testament data which bear witness to such conditions
as ignorance, developing consciousness of his mission, and the
terrible abandonment on the Cross which exegesis has been able
to establish as historical aspects of the life of Jesus.[9]

From this it is obvious that as long as a metaphysical
Christology works in a vacuum it cannot present an understanding of Christ which adequately deals with the concerns raised by
these other two branches of theology.

2.1.2.2. *Prejudicial Sources of the Problem*

In addition to the methodological sources of the problem,
there is the problem of a basic monophysite bias both in metaphysical Christology and in popular thinking about Christ.
Rahner perceives this bias and rather consistently warns of its
consequences for Christology.[10] Despite the fact that this Christology is formally and verbally correct, it rather consistently
downplays the significance of the human nature of Christ. As
far as the popular mentality is concerned, in its *de facto* perception of Christ it imagines him as some kind of *tertium quid*, as
God "disguised" as a man, but with very little appreciation of
the reality of the human nature of Christ. On a theoretical level
this bias presents itself primarily in discussions of the know-

---

⁹ *Ibid.*, pp. 149-163; *idem*, "The Position of Christology in the Church
between Exegesis and Dogmatics," *TI* XI, pp. 185-214; *idem*, "Bemerkungen
zur Bedeutung der Geschichte Jesu für die katholische Dogmatik,"
Schriften X, pp. 215-218.

¹⁰ Cf. "Current Problems in Christology," *TI* I, pp. 155-161, esp. p. 156,
note 2, and p. 160, note 2; "On the Theology of the Incarnation," *TI* IV,
p. 117f.; "Christology Within an Evolutionary World View," *TI* V, p. 176f.;
"The Position of Christology in the Church between Exegesis and Dogmatics," *TI* XI, p. 197f. By monophysite we mean that position which seeks
to explain the unity of Christ's Person by positing only one nature of
him, a divine nature; because it denies the true humanity of Jesus, this
position is clearly heretical. While the popular mentality and classic
school theologies are *not* heretical, they do exhibit a tendency, a bias, in
a monophysite manner.

ledge and freedom of the human will of Christ. On a popular level it evidences itself in ways of thinking and praying that are an effective denial of the statement of the Letter to the Hebrews that Jesus "has been tempted as we are, yet without sin (4:15)."

The cause of this bias is to be found in the concern of Christology to avoid the pitfalls of Arianism. Thus theologians assume the fact that Christ had a human nature and are concerned to emphasize his divinity. However, in explaining the relationship of the two natures in the one person of Christ, the human nature consistently suffers being downplayed to the point where one could ask if that human nature existentially and effectively continues to be of any real meaning. The results of this bias are disastrous, because instead of firmly anchoring the Incarnation in both human nature and human history, theology ends up presenting a picture of Christ which seems frankly mythological to men of our age.[11]

The awareness of these problems on the horizon of understanding of the Chalcedonian formula on the relationship of the two natures in the one person of Christ has strongly influenced Rahner's Christological writings. Much of what he says is his own attempt to provide a correction for both the methodological and prejudicial problems involved. We will now analyze Rahner's attempts to allow the full reality of the human nature of Christ to be truly, existentially functional. We will see in this analysis how Rahner has attempted to overcome the methodological problem by applying his understanding of man to the Jesus of the Gospels, thereby firmly anchoring the Incarnation in human nature and human history, and thus avoiding the problem of a monophysite bias.

2.1.3.0. THE ONTOLOGICAL BASIS OF THE UNION: THE INCARNATION AND ANTHROPOLOGY

The starting point for a metaphysical Christology is the statement, "The Word of God became man," and this is also Rahner's starting point.[12] Rahner locates the basic problematic in a proper understanding of the predicate "man." The theologian must first determine the meaning of man if he wishes to predicate humanity of the Logos. We are thus transported into the field of a theological anthropology, i.e., an understanding of what

---

[11] "On the Theology of the Incarnation," *TI* IV, p. 117f.
[12] *Ibid.*, p. 105f.

man is in light of revelation, an understanding which must deal
with man's openness to God, and thereby establish the anthropological conditions for the possibility of the event we call Incarnation.

A theological anthropology, according to Rahner, is composed of two basic elements: *first*, an *a posteriori* element in
which the data of Revelation concerning man and his relationship to God (i.e., his creatureliness, his covenant relationship
with God, his position as addressee of Revelation, the fact of the
Incarnation as the absolute and irreversible culmination of Revelation, man's vocation to glory in the vision of God) are col-
lected together as the material for the *second* element, an *a priori*
transcendental reflection, whose goal is to establish the ontological conditions necessary for man to be involved in this relationship to God.[13]

This anthropologically orientated Christology is not an attempt to escape from the necessity of speaking about God and
the supernatural. Rather, it is born of the urgent necessity of
doing just that, but of doing it in such a way that God and the
supernatural are seen precisely as the ground of the existence
of this world and of man in particular. Only by approaching the
problem from this point of view can God be understood as
having an essential, intrinsic relationship to the world, and hence
man can be seen as having an essential and intrinsic relationship
to God. Without such a Christian anthropology the reality of
God and his grace remains extrinsic, so that man could then
realize his humanity in complete indifference to God.

> ... anthropology and Christology mutually determine each other
> within Christian dogmatics if they are both correctly under-
> stood. Christian anthropology is only able to fulfill its whole
> purpose if it understands man as the *potentia oboedientialis*
> for the "Hypostatic Union." And Christology can only be un-
> dertaken from the point of view of this kind of transcendental
> anthropology; for in order to say today what the "Hypostatic
> Union" is without being suspected of merely reproducing no
> longer feasible "mythologies," the idea of the God-man needs
> proof of a transcendental orientation in man's being and history
> under grace. A purely *a posteriori* Christology, unable to in-

---

[13] Rahner and Vorgrimmler, "Anthropologie," *Kleines theologisches
Wörterbuch* (Freiburg: Herder, 1961), p. 23f.; *ibid.*, "Mensch," p. 238; *idem.*,
"Anthropologie: III-theologisch," *Sacramentum Mundi* I (Freiburg: Herder,
1968), col. 176-186; *idem.*, "Mensch: III-Zum theologischen Begriff des
Menschen," *Sacramentum Mundi* III (Freiburg: Herder, 1969), col. 407-417.

tegrate Christology correctly into an evolutionary total view of the world, would not find it easy to dismiss the suspicion of propounding mythology.[14]

And so we are faced with a double task. According to Rahner the ontological basis for the Incarnation must be sought in an anthropology which defines man in such a way that this human reality is capable of being assumed by God in a possible Incarnation; and this understanding of man must be integrated into a total world view. We will now discuss Rahner's writings on anthropology and Christology from this double point of view.

2.1.3.1. *The Meaning of Man*

Rahner's starting point for a theological definition of man is the fact that man is precisely the undefinable. He cannot express the fulness of his being in a categorical definition. He knows many things about himself, but he can never adequately define his essence, "... for one can only say what man is by expressing what he is concerned with and what is concerned with him."[15] Because these "concerns" are unlimited, man experiences himself as a mystery. Not the absolute mystery itself, but as "mystery in his real being and its ultimate reason, in his nature, which is the humble, conscious state of being referred to the fulness ...."[16] This is the closest Rahner comes to defining man: *the humble, conscious state of being referred to the fulness.*

Thus we can only properly comprehend man if we understand him as having his nature precisely in this reference to the fulness of the absolute mystery which is God. This understanding of man becomes historically concrete in each individual human life in the basic *act* of each man, which is "... the acceptance or rejection of the mystery which we are, as we find our poverty referred to the mystery of the fulness."[17] Rahner points out that at this point we must have a clear understanding of what we mean by mystery. Mystery is not the "undiscovered unknown," nor is it the "only provisionally" unmastered; rather, mystery is "... the impenetrable which is already present and does not need to be fetched ...." This mystery is present as

---

[14] Rahner, "Theology and Anthropology," *TI* IX, pp. 28f.
[15] Rahner, "On the Theology of the Incarnation," *TI* IV, p. 108.
[16] *Ibid.*, p. 108.
[17] *Ibid.*, p. 108.

the "... horizon of all understanding." [18]   It is the fundamental
characteristic of the relationship between God and man, and
it is this so radically that even in the direct vision of God which
is promised us as the fulfillment of our being, God remains the
incomprehensible mystery. [19]

On the basis of these considerations Rahner proceeds to
identify this description of man with the *potentia oboedientialis*:
« ... it means that this *potentia* is not one potentiality along with
other possibilities in the constituent elements of human nature:
it is objectively identical with the essence of man." [20]   Thus man
fulfills his essence to the degree that this potentiality is realized
in the act of surrendering himself into the mystery of God. [21]

This theological understanding of man in terms of *potentia
oboedientialis* is the ontological foundation for considering the
possibility of the Incarnation. For the *possibility* of God becoming man, of making his own the reality of a human nature without destroying or doing violence to that human nature is grounded
precisely in the fact that man is, by definition, the openness to
God.

Two important clarifications are necessary here:

1. This theological consideration of the nature of man establishes that one of the possible ways in which his transcendence
to God can be fulfilled is for that human nature itself to be
assumed by God. This *a priori* consideration does not thereby
necessitate an Incarnation in order that this transcendence find
its fulfillment.

2. We know from Revelation that this possibility has been
fulfilled. But this does not mean that Incarnation must be
realized in every being who has this nature. [22]

---

[18] *Ibid.*, p. 108.

[19] *Ibid.*, p. 108f.

[20] *Ibid.*, p. 110. We reproduce here the definition of *potentia oboedientialis* from Rahner and Vorgrimmler, *Concise Theological Dictionary*
(London: Burns & Oates, 1965), p. 367: "The intrinsic being of man is
called an "obediential potency" for supernatural graces insofar as in
virtue of his spiritual transcendence to all being, man is open to God's
self-communication, which can only be imparted to a creature whose nature does not confine it to a particular sphere of existence. This potency
(receptivity) is called "obediential" because what it really is would still
be meaningful if God did not communicate himself; so that this communication remains free notwithstanding the potency — that is, remains
grace. The potency has no claims to advance before God but remains
obedient to his good pleasure."

[21] *Ibid.*, p. 109-110.

[22] *Ibid.*, pp. 110-111.

Thus Rahner has shown that there exists in human nature the transcendental possibility of being predicated of God, as in the statement, "The Word of God became a man." The existence of this human possibility in no way detracts from the freedom of God in deciding to realize this possibility, nor does its realization necessitate that it occur in every human being. In this way the Incarnation remains God's free act, and Jesus of Nazareth remains the unique historical occurrence of this act on the part of God.

Rahner's concern is to state the "... ontological counterpart to the ontic statements of tradition ...." [23] It is his attempt to state the tradition in such a way that the monophysite bias can be avoided. To that extent we can consider it successful, because it takes the total reality of the being of man and understands it in such a way that nothing in that nature must be sacrificed or short-changed in order to predicate it of God in the Incarnation. The human nature of Jesus Christ is precisely that openness to God which is common to all men. It is that same openness to God realized in a perfect way, because in freedom it opens itself completely to accept the action of the Word upon it. In doing this, Jesus is the perfect fulfillment of what it means to be truly man. And in saying this, we have come full circle — just as the starting point was the search for the meaning of man, in Christ we arrive at the full and complete actualization of human being.

2.1.3.2. *Anthropology and Evolution: Integration into a World Wiew*

If this theological anthropology is necessary to avoid the danger of a monophysite bias, the integration of this understanding of man into the dominant contemporary world-view of evolutionary theory is equally necessary to avoid the danger of appearing mythological when we speak of the Incarnation.

Rahner assumes that the generally accepted world-view of our day is evolutionary in character, and without involving himself in any particular theory of evolution he isolates five points where this world-view and Christian theology converge:

1) The world, material and spiritual is the creation of God. The variety of beings in the world has its one cause in God, and

---

[23] *Ibid.*, p. 111.

that variety itself forms "... a unity in origin, self-realization and determination ...." [24]

2) The unity of this variety shows itself most clearly in man. The unity of matter and spirit is fundamental and is prior to any subsequent division or differentiation into elements. [25]

3) Science knows the properties of matter, but not matter itself. This experience of matter leads science back to the question of man himself. Man experiences matter as the principle of individuation by which he experiences the world as "other" in time and space. In relation to this really distinct "other" man achieves the possibilities of his own existence by the exercise of his freedom. [26]

4) The evolution of matter is a process of self-transcendence which results not merely in something "other"; this other is also "more." This process of becoming more takes place in relation to God who is the fulness of Being, and in relation to man as self-conscious. [27]

5) Man is "the self-transcendence of living matter." Matter develops toward him and is subsumed into his history. Thus his history is not only spiritual (i.e., culture), but also material (i.e., transformation of matter by technology). The consummation of the world as the goal of history takes place in him. [28]

From these considerations we can see that both theology and evolutionary thought have man as a central focus of their respective teachings. Thus this convergence on certain key points is to be expected. Theology sees man as the crown of God's creation, and evolutionary theory sees the achievement of hominization as the breakthrough to a new level of being. How evolutionary theory interprets hominization can lead to a major parting of the ways between the two fields of knowledge. Theology must insist that man is the goal of Nature, the point at which Nature has achieved self-consciousness. Any explanation of this achievement as the result of mere chance must be rejected. Furthermore, theology must insist that man himself has a goal. His existence is not imperiled, nor is it orientated

---

[24] Rahner, "Christology Within an Evolutionary View of the World," *TI* V, p. 161.

[25] *Ibid.*, p. 161f.

[26] *Ibid.*, p. 162f.

[27] *Ibid.*, p. 164ff.

[28] *Ibid.*, p. 168.

toward a return to some primordial state; rather the goal of man is essentially bound up with the immortality of the human soul.[29]

What Rahner is trying to clarify here is the understanding of the anthropocentric character of modern thought. Both theology and evolutionary theory understand the world in its relation to man. The cosmos finds its highest expression in man. It is man who brings Nature to itself via his own self-consciousness. What theology must insist upon, however, is that man himself can only be understood in relation to God. In and through man the cosmos is seen in its fundamental theocentric character — God is the origin and end of the cosmos.

With this view of man and human history in mind, Rahner undertakes to show how Christology can be understood as having a place within the broader context of the Creator-creation relationship.[30] Everything outside of God is the result of his will to communicate himself to what is other than himself. Thus creation itself is the calling into existence of this other, the first step in achieving this goal. The creation of man in particular is the positing of a subject capable of freely receiving and accepting this self-communication of God. Because man is part of the cosmos, i.e., because he is a being whose existence is posited in spatial-temporal categories, this self-communication of God, in order to be received and accepted by man, must itself take place in space and time. Thus revelation must be historical. As a result, the history of the cosmos and salvation history are coextensive.[31] Rahner uses these data of creation-revelation and evolution to transcendentally deduce the *idea* of what a Saviour would be: he is *both* the self-communication of God himself and the free human-creaturely acceptance of this communication.[32]

This transcendental deduction of the *idea* of a Saviour enables Rahner to clarify the relationship between the doctrine

---

[29] *Ibid.*, pp. 169-173. Cf. also Rahner, "Hominisation", *Quaestiones Disputatae* 13, transl. W. T. O'Hara (New York: Herder and Herder, 1965), esp. Chapter III, pp. 45-109.

[30] Rahner classifies this as a basically Scotist view. Cf. *ibid.*, pp. 184-185. It is also one of the fundamental principles of his own Christology: Cf. "Current Problems in Christology," *TI* I, pp. 163-165; "Christology in the Setting of Modern Man's Understanding of Himself and of His World," *TI* XI, pp. 223-225. Hereafter cited as "Christology in the Setting..."

[31] *Ibid.*, p. 173f. Cf. also *Hörer des Wortes*, Chapters 10-13, pp. 150-202.

[32] *Ibid.*, p. 174f.

of the Incarnation *as* Hypostatic Union and an evolutionary
world-view. This involves two basic considerations:

1) "... the Saviour is himself a historical moment in God's
saving action exercised on the world." This means that the
Saviour is a part of the cosmos and its history. Thus he is
truly a man. He is a true Incarnation into humanity, i.e., the
creation and acceptance of human reality "... *as his* own reality."
Thus the human, historical appearance of the Saviour is not a
costume, as monophysitism would have it, nor is it a relationship
only to the spiritual element in man, as gnosticism teaches. The
Saviour is historically a man.[33]

2) *This* notion of a Saviour implies the Hypostatic Union.
This implication, however, needs clarification. Is the Hypostatic
Union simply a step in evolution which has been achieved in
only one single case, so that all other men are simply non-evolved?
Or is it truly a breakthrough in an evolutionary sense, so that
it does indeed have effects for the whole human race? Rahner
insists that we must answer "No" to the first question and "Yes"
to the second if Christology and evolution are to be compatible.
What, then, are the effects on the human race? Rahner answers
by saying that the effects of the Hypostatic Union on the human
nature of Christ are the same as the goal of all mankind, viz.,
the direct vision of God.[34] The Hypostatic Union is indeed
unique; but by placing it within the broader context of creation
and human history, it may be seen as a constitutive element,
"... an intrinsic factor of the whole process of the bestowal of
grace on the spiritual creature in general."[35] Because the cosmos
and human history *are* at the same time creation and salvation
history, the Hypostatic Union can be understood in an evolutionary context as the point where man's transcendence into the
Absolute Being of God and God's absolute self-communication
to man converge.

Hence we arrive at Rahner's definition of the Hypostatic
Union:

> Hypostatic Union "... means this and nothing else: in the human
> reality of Jesus, God's absolute saving purpose (the absolute
> event of God's self-communication to us) is simply, absolutely
> and irrevocably present; in it is present both the declaration
> made to us and its acceptance — something effected by God

---

[33] *Ibid.*, p. 176f.
[34] *Ibid.*, pp. 178-181.
[35] *Ibid.*, p. 181.

himself, a reality of God himself, unmixed and yet inseparable and hence irrevocable. This declaration, however, is the pledge of grace to us.[36]

2.1.3.3. *Some Clarifications*

At this point some clarifications are in order. We must remember that Rahner's starting point is the Chalcedonian definition of the Hypostatic Union in which a true human nature is predicated of the Word of God in the Incarnation. The first question to be asked, then, was: What do we understand by man? This led to the discussion of theological anthropology. The second question was how this theological anthropology fits in with the general, anthropological viewpoint of contemporary evolutionary thought. In both cases the discussion centered on an *a priori*, transcendental deduction of the ontological conditions of the possibility of predicating humanity of the Logos in such a way that the demands of the Chalcedonian definition may be met.

In addition to calling attention to the starting point, two other clarifications, which Rahner himself makes, must be kept in mind. First, if we have transcendentally deduced the idea of a God-man from these considerations, this does not mean that the concept of faith has been eliminated. The fact that Jesus of Nazareth *is* this God-man can only be accepted in faith.[37] Christology must deal with the history of Jesus of Nazareth, as clarified by exegesis and fundamental theology, to show that the object of faith is this historical person, and not some transcendental idea.[38]

The second clarification is that this transcendental deduction must perceive the processes by which man transcends himself into the power of God and by which God communicates himself to man as both occurring, radically and fundamentally, in the power of God. Thus the convergence of the two in some point in history (i.e., in the history of Jesus of Nazareth) is not the result of some ineluctable, blind process. It is, rather, the "fulness of time" willed by God in the very act of communicating himself to the "other" by creating that "other." [39]

---

[36] *Ibid.*, p. 183f.

[37] *Ibid.*, p. 188.

[38] Cf. Rahner, "Christology in the Setting ..." *TI* XI, p. 225f.; *idem*, "Bemerkungen zur Bedeutung der Geschichte Jesu für die katholische Dogmatic," *Schriften* X, p. 215f.

[39] *Ibid.*, p. 226f.

2.1.4.0. THE PERSONAL-EXISTENTIAL BASIS OF THE UNION: THE KNOWLEDGE AND SELF-CONSCIOUSNESS OF CHRIST

The general ontological considerations which were part of Rahner's *a priori* transcendental consideration of the conditions necessary for a Hypostatic Union enter the personal-existential sphere where he considers the concrete historical person of Jesus in terms of his knowledge and self-consciousness. As we saw in our discussion of the problems in understanding, this issue is pertinent to both the methodological problems and the bias of much of traditional Christology. It is the point at which biblical, fundamental and dogmatic theology converge. It is also the point where the ontic, ontological and existential statements converge in the historical person of Jesus of Nazareth. It is perhaps the most concrete standard we have to judge the adequacy of any Christology in terms of the Chalcedonian dialectic.

Historically, theology has dealt with the question of the knowledge and self-consciousness of Christ from two points of view. One position sees the question in terms of moral necessity. Jesus must have this *visio Dei* and this infused knowledge in order to fulfill his function as divine legate who speaks with authority.[40] The second position views this question in terms of ontological necessity. Because of the Hypostatic Union, the human nature of Christ must be conscious of its ontological determination by the Logos. What is ontologically higher determines what is ontologically lower; hence the human consciousness of Christ must be aware of that determination. Thus the *visio* is an intrinsic element of the Union itself, and this *visio* is conceived of in terms of the highest degree of beatitude which the human soul can possess.[41]

Basically Rahner's position would agree with the ontological viewpoint. However, he is seeking to arrive at an understanding of the problem of the knowledge and self-consciousness of Christ which is theologically more differentiated in light of the data of the Scriptures as these have been interpreted by modern exegesis and biblical theology, and in light of contemporary philosophy's understanding of human knowledge.

---

[40] Rahner, "Dogmatic Reflections on the Knowledge and Self-Consciousness of Christ," *TI* V, p. 204.

[41] *Ibid.*, p. 204ff. Cf. L. Billot, *De Verbo Incarnato*, 9th ed. (Rome: PUG, 1949), p. 177ff.

He begins his discussion by criticising what he calls "... the tacit presupposition that man's knowing consciousness is the famous *tabula rasa* on which something is either written or not ...." [42] This either-or proposition simply does not fit the facts of human consciousness as we ourselves experience it. Human consciousness is a complex of subjective and objective experiences, of reflected and unreflected data, of implicit and explicit propositions. Among these data there is "... an *a priori* unobjectified knowledge about oneself, and this is a basic condition of the spiritual subject...." [43] This state of being aware of oneself, however, is not an object of knowledge itself and, even when man reflects upon it, it can never become completely thematic.

Rahner premises his discussion with a second criticism of "... the Greek ideal of man in which knowledge is simply the yard-stick of human nature as such." [44] Thus the lack of knowledge in man is considered an imperfection, a negative characteristic which must be overcome. Rahner contrasts this view of nescience with the view of a contemporary philosophy in which nescience has a positive quality in its influence on and challenge to the individual to launch himself into the unknown in which the human being can realize himself by his own free decision. [45]

This brings us to the central question of this issue:

> ... for what reasons must one, together with Catholic text-book theology and the *magisterium*, ascribe to Jesus even during his life on earth the kind of direct vision of God which is the basis and centre of the beatific vision of God enjoyed by the blessed in heaven? [46]

What Rahner is asking here is this: Granted that we concede that the basis of the vision in Christ and in all men in a state of glory is the same, must we therefore concede that the immediate vision of God which Jesus had during his earthly life was *eo ipso* a *beatific vision*? This is in fact two questions. First, we have the question of the anthropological basis of a direct presence to God in a Hypostatic Union; second, we have

---

[42] Rahner, "Dogmatic Reflections on the Knowledge and Self-Consciousness of Christ," *TI* V, p. 200.

[43] *Ibid.*, p. 200.

[44] *Ibid.*, p. 201.

[45] *Ibid.*, p. 202.

[46] *Ibid.*, p. 202.

the question of how this direct presence to God is to be conceived when confronted with the historical data about Jesus.

We have already seen Rahner's basis for answering the first
question. The basic openness to Being in a process of transcendence whereby man realizes himself reaches its highest actualization in the Hypostatic Union. Because his human nature is
ontically joined to the divine nature in Hypostatic Union, ontologically one of the unthematic data of Jesus' self-consciousness
must be this condition of direct presence to God. The ontic
condition of being Son of God must have its ontological effects
on the human consciousness of Jesus, but in that same unthematic way in which all men achieve self-consciousness. Thus
without prejudice either to Jesus' human consciousness or to
his unique state of being hypostatically united with the Logos,
Rahner can posit that same real development and growth in
Jesus' consciousness which is characteristic of all men.[47]

When we apply this first consideration to the second question, Rahner insists that we remain in the realm of the subjective categories of self-consciousness in which the whole discussion has taken place. If self-consciousness is a subjective, unthematic, fundamental experience of the unity of one's own being, then we should not suddenly switch over to objective, thematic categories when we speak of the self-consciousness of
Christ. The experience of direct presence to God which the
human nature of Jesus has because of the Hypostatic Union is
precisely this subjective, unthematic self-awareness. Thus all
explanations of this phenomenon which consciously or uncon-
sciously use the imaginary model of Jesus looking at himself as
in a mirror and seeing the Logos in the reflected image are

---

[47] *Ibid.*, p. 206. We have here a good example of the distinction, which
is fundamental to Rahner's thought, between *ontic* and *ontological*. Ontic
refers to Being *in se*, in its constitutive moments. *Ontological* refers to
Being *as known*. Because of the transcendental character of Being, there
is a correspondence between the ontic and the ontological. Rahner's
concept of analogy is based on this distinction. The degree of "having
being" is based on the degree of the relationship between a Being's
"knowability" and its actual "being known." It is a fact of human knowing that this dialectic cannot be completely resolved. Thus man's concepts, based on "being known," never completely and adequately exhaust
the content of the ontic level of Being *in se*. There is always an outstanding "MORE" which eludes man in his knowedge of Being. Cf. *Geist
in Welt, passim.* This outstanding "MORE" is at the core of man's experience of himself as "openness to the fulness of the mystery." Cf.
Hörer des Wortes, esp. pp. 71-88.

mistaken precisely because they have made this conversion into objective categories. Rahner insists that the self-consciousness of Jesus as hypostatically united to the Logos is not an object of knowledge. It is an unthematic data of his self-awareness. [48].

Rahner insists that it is this understanding of the problem which is open to deal with the Jesus of the Gospels, the Jesus "... who questions, doubts, learns, is surprised, is deeply moved, ... who is overwhelmed by a deadly feeling of being forsaken by God." [49] Thus the vision is *direct*, and hence the same for Christ's human nature as it is for those in a state of glory. But it is not *beatific* if one understands that term as excluding all real suffering and sorrow. The experiences of Jesus in the Gospels are real, human experiences. In and through them he truly grows and develops in his consciousness of himself and his mission. The ontic Union is "... really present in its fullest being" precisely in this subjective experience of the human consciousness of Jesus as being united with the Logos. [50]

In our judgment we can discern in Rahner's thought on this problem a particular application of the functioning of the Chalcedonian dialectic. The human consciousness of Christ is "undivided" from the Logos; it is precisely the ontic fact of the Union which causes the consciousness of being Son of God. It is at the same time "unmixed," it is not some kind of *tertium quid* consciousness; it is a true, human consciousness such as is generally experienced by all men. In fact, Rahner himself appeals to dialectical thought to point out that it is

> "... meaningful ... to attribute to Jesus at the same time an absolute, basic state of being directly present to God from the very beginning and a development of this original self-consciousness of the created spiritual nature being absolutely handed over to the Logos. For this development does not refer to the establishment of the basic state of direct presence to God but to the objective, humanly and conceptually expressed articulation and objectification of this basic state; this basic condition is not a fully formed and propositionally differentiated knowledge, nor is it an *objective* vision.[51]

On the basis of this same understanding of *visio immediata* Rahner addresses the problem of the infused knowledge of Chirst.

---

[48] *Ibid.*, p. 207.
[49] *Ibid.*, p. 207.
[50] *Ibid.*, p. 207.
[51] *Ibid.*, p. 211.

He seems to use as his starting point Gutwenger's assertion that there is no compelling theological reason to ascribe a *scientia infusa* to Christ in addition to acquired human knowledge and the *visio immediata*. [52]   Rahner says it is sufficient to explain an infused knowledge in Christ in terms of the process by which the *visio Dei*, which is part of Christ's human consciousness, becomes ever more reflected, objective knowledge.   Thus we can understand this infused knowledge as a habitual state of Christ's human intellect without requiring "an immense number of individual '*species infusae*,' but it could be conceived as an *a priori* basis for a knowledge developing through the encounter with the world of experience." [53]

2.1.5.0.   EVALUATION: THE UNITY OF CHRIST'S EXPERIENCE WITH OURS

In this first section we have given a brief description of Rahner's thought on the Hypostatic Union.   We have seen that his starting point and hermeneutical principle is the definition of the Council of Chalcedon.   Much of his own thought springs from what he considers to be the failure of much of school-theology to appreciate the dialectic of the Chalcedonian definition.   While these theologies are verbally correct, they betray a fairly consistent pattern of downplaying the human aspect of the dialectic in order to accentuate the divine.   Thus they bear within themselves the seeds of monophysite and docetic misunderstandings that have often become evident in the popular, average Christian understanding of Jesus Christ.

It is against this background that Rahner sets out to theologize about the Hypostatic Union and avoid the pitfalls of traditional Christology.   He begins by asserting that if God becomes man, there must be some characteristic of man that enables him to be assumed by God as his own reality in the world.   This led us to discuss the anthropological basis of the Hypostatic Union.   This theological anthropology is of such a nature that it opens into a Christology, and a Christology must show that Hypostatic Union is the ultimate of human possibilities without detracting from the gratuity of the Union actually occurring. This anthropology was then seen to be compatible with the gen-

---

[52] *Ibid.,* p. 212.   Cf. E. Gutwenger, *Bewusstsein und Wissen Christi* (Innsbruck: Rauch, 1960).

[53] *Ibid.,* p. 213.

eral evolutionary world-view of our times by placing it within the broader context of a Creator-creature and a salvation history-history relationship. The understanding of the Hypostatic Union becomes most personally experiential (both for Christ and for us) in the discussion of the biblical data on the knowledge and self-consciousness of Christ in terms of this anthropology.

If the Chalcedonian dialectic is his starting point and his hermeneutical principle when confronting traditional Christologies, it is also functionally operative in Rahner's own Christology. God creates the world as "other" in order to reveal himself, and in the culminating act of revelation he himself becomes a real part of that "other" by assuming a human nature. Thus the Logos truly *becomes* man, "like us in all things but sin." This is Rahner's most radical break with traditional Christology, but he insists that if it is understood properly in a dialectical sense, it no more involves a denial of the immutability of God than the profession of faith in the Trinity involves a denial of the unity of God. [54]

Rahner's aim in his discussion of the Hypostatic Union is to allow the true, full humanity of Christ to be conceptually and existentially operative in theology and in the "catechism of the heart" of all Christians. In terms of a "Christology from above," if one keeps the functional dialectic in mind, we would judge this attempt a successful one, for he has shown that Christ's human experience, although unique and insurpassable because of the Hypostatic Union, is basically one with ours. All those dynamic, existential elements which contemporary man experiences at the root of his being and in terms of which he knows himself to be man — all these elements are present in the humanity of Jesus, all except sin.

2.2.0. THE WORK OF CHRIST: MEDIATORSHIP

In this section we will present Rahner's critique of traditional soteriology and his own soteriological statements which he derives from the understanding of Hypostatic Union which we saw in the previous section. We may preface this considera-

---

[54] Rahner, "On the Theology of the Incarnation," *TI* IV, p. 113f., note 3. On this point cf. G. McCool, *A Rahner Reader* (New York: Seabury, 1975), p. 145f; W. Shepherd, *Man's Condition* (New York: Herder and Herder, 1969), p. 199; T. Pearl, "Dialectical Panentheism: On the Hegelian Character of Karl Rahner's Key Christological Writings," *I Th Q* 42 (1975), pp. 119-137.

tion by saying that what we are concerned to do is to explicate Rahner's tastement: "We understand his [Christ's] true nature only when we see it as absolutely one with his function in saving history." [55]

2.2.1.0. RAHNER'S CRITIQUE OF TRADITIONAL SOTERIOLOGY

We will discuss Rahner's critique of traditional soteriology in three parts, acording to what that soteriology has to say about the life of Christ, his passion and death, and his resurrection as they pertain to the salvation of mankind.[56] Rahner is concerned to show that a biased understanding of the Hypostatic Union, when combined with a purely formal interest in the value of the redemptive, vicarious satisfaction offered by Christ, results in an impoverished understanding of the meaning of the redemption, both for Christ and for us.

2.2.1.1. *Traditional Soteriology and the Life of Christ*

For the traditional soteriology of the schools, the events of the life of Christ, beyond the fact of the Incarnation and the passion, are not discussed as having redemptive significance. This state of affairs derives from a point of view which says that since the value of Jesus' acts depends on the value they receive because of the Hypostatic Union, i.e., an infinite value, any one of these acts could be redemptive in itself, provided that God accepts it as such. This formal point of view is correct in itself. But because the redemption in the concrete was wrought by the passion and death of Christ, traditional soteriology has focused its attention on these events alone. Thus the events of the life of Christ have been seen as the "stuff" of meditation and as examples of abstract moral teaching, but their soteriological significance has been largely ignored.[57]

---

[55] Rahner, "The Position of Christology ...," *TI* XI, p. 204.

[56] Inasmuch as these are all events in the history of Jesus of Nazareth, this division is formal and artificial. It seems justified, however, by the statements (and the silence) about these three "phases" in traditional soteriology.

[57] Cf. Rahner, "Current Problems in Christology," *TI* I, p. 190ff.

2.2.1.2. *Traditional Soteriology and the Death of Christ*

While the traditional soteriology of the schools, in accord with the teaching of the Church, has maintained the soteriological significance of the death of Christ on the Cross, the focus for discussing the redemptive merit of his death is shifted to the suffering which preceded the death. This shift can be explained because of theology's formal interest in the sacrificial nature of the atonement offered to God by Christ, and derives from viewing the death of Christ in formal moral categories. Also at play in this understanding of Christ's death is the notion of death itself, i.e., death understood simply in terms of the separation of the body and the soul. Thus the passion of Christ is the cause of this merit, and death is a consequence of the passion.

In this view there is no understanding of the significance of death in itself as an *act* of human life.[58] It would seem that in this view of the death of Christ, the answer to the question, "Why did Jesus die?" is simply stated in terms of its redemptive merit, "To save all men"; what is missing is precisely the answer that would be given of any other person's death, viz., "Because he was a man and all men die." With its emphasis on the preternatural gifts of Christ's human nature, and because of the way in which it explains the nature of the Hypostatic Union, traditional soteriology itself reveals the same monophysite bias which Rahner criticizes in traditional Christology.

2.2.1.3. *Traditional Soteriology and the Resurrection*

Despite the fact that the resurrection of Christ is the central point of Christian faith, Rahner criticizes traditional soteriology for practically ignoring the soteriological significance of this event. It appears either as an epilogue to the saving act of Christ's death, or it is given no soteriological meaning of its own.[59] Thus the resurrection is seen as a kind of personal reward to the humanity of Jesus, as a model of baptism and the general resurrection of the dead, and as an apologetical proof of prime importance. It is not seen as having any causal link with the redemption, nor does the glorified humanity of Christ appear to have any effects on his role as mediator for all eternity.[60]

---

[58] *Ibid.*, pp. 192-197; *idem.*, "Dogmatic Questions on Easter," *TI* IV, p. 127f.

[59] Rahner, "Dogmatic Questions on Easter," *TI* IV, p. 127f.

[60] Cf. L. Ott, *op. cit.*, p. 192f. for a good illustration of this point of view.

2.2.2.0. RAHNER'S SOTERIOLOGY

In addressing ourselves to Rahner's soteriology we must necessarily keep in mind all that we said in the previous section on Hypostatic Union. At the same time this presentation will deepen our understanding of the fundamental conclusion we drew from that discussion, viz., that Christ's experience and ours are fundamentally the same.

2.2.2.1. *Human Reality as the Reality of God: The Redemption of Man*

The question from which Rahner proceeds is the same question of traditional theology. What is the significance of the death of Jesus Christ? If Jesus is truly man as well as truly God, the significance of death for his human nature must be fundamentally the same as it is for all men. And so we are faced with the more fundamental question of the meaning of death in general. Theologically this question has been dealt with in the following terms:

— death is the separation of the soul and the body;
— death is a consequence of sin;
— death is the end of the *status viae* in terms of moral merit.[61]

Each of these statements is valid, but they do not exhaust the possibilities. If we shift our anthropology from a static point of view in which man's nature is something which is given, a fixed essence, to a dynamic point of view in which man's nature is something which he realizes in the process of his life, then death takes on a deeper existential meaning. This is the background for Rahner's reinterpretation of death.

Traditionally death has been looked upon as a purely passive event, something which man undergoes. It is the end of life as we know it in this world. Rahner maintains that this view is inadequate. If we take man's nature as spirit and matter, as spirit which realizes itself in and through its personal and free decisions and actions which express themselves externally in the body, then the reason *why* death is the end of the time of meriting becomes more evident. Death is not only something which man undergoes; it is the final act of his life. It is the act by

---

61 Cf. *DS* 1512; 838; 856; 925; 1000; 1304; 1488.

which all that he has become by his free action in this world is summed up and expressed in a final, irrevocable way. Thus death is not something which merely affects the body. It is itself an act of the whole man; it is an act in which his soul, his spiritual nature, is playing an active role. There is in death, then, a dialectic of action and passion, and it is precisely this dialectic which gives death its mysterious, inscrutable character.[62]

If death has this final, expressive characteristic, then the relationship between life and death can be seen more clearly. The actions of a life are orientated toward the final act of life, the act of dying. That act of dying itself expresses in a summary way what the meaning of the individual actions of a lifetime is. These are formal, ontological considerations which are derived from the nature of man, and they are valid for every human death, quite apart from any (strictly) theological interpretations of the fact of death itself. Thus it is not strictly necessary to first accept the theological interpretation of death as a consequence of sin in order to accept Rahner's interpretation of death as the final act of life.

From this consideration Rahner gains a deeper insight into the death of Christ. As a consequence of the Hypostatic Union, the Logos became truly man. This means he assumed a human nature, a human history, and hence a human life and death. His death is esentially similar to the death of all men.[63] And because of the expressive nature of death itself we come to understand precisely *why* it was through his *death* that Jesus redeemed all mankind, and here Rahner goes beyond the traditional theory of satisfaction. Death is not merely one moral act among others. It is *the* act in which the mystery of man as it is expressed in action and passion throughout the whole process of life is present to man in a unique way as the object of his freedom. Thus for Christ, as for us, the act of dying is the fullest expression of what we have become, of what we are as the result of our lives, before God and man. From this we can see precisely why it is this act of dying, in which Christ expresses and summarizes what he *is* in obedience and love, and passively surrenders all to the Father, which is in itself the final revelation of what Christ is and at the same time the act by which we are redeemed.[64]

---

[62] Cf. Rahner, "On the Theology of Death," *Quaestiones Disputatae* 2 (New York: Herder and Herder, 1961), pp. 13-31, and p. 40.

[63] *Ibid.*, p. 57.

[64] *Ibid.*, pp. 58-62.

From this perspective of the meaning of death as a human act, Rahner is able to say something about the soteriological meaning of Christ's life. Death is "... an axiological factor which dominates the whole of life ...." [65] This means that the real value of individual actions of human life is understood properly in relationship to the final, morally conclusive act of dying, and this act of dying itself is the summation of the value of those individual acts. We have seen in this discussion why in assuming a human nature it is to be expected that the Logos should also assume a human death as an intrinsic element of that nature, and why it is the act of death alone which has the meaning proper to a single act which can have redemptive significance. From the axiological unity of life and death Rahner draws some conclusions about the redemptive meaning of Christ's life. First of all, he disagrees with the opinion of the satisfaction theory that any act of Christ's life could have been redemptive. [66] Only death as a human act has the qualities necessary for the *one* act which can truly be redemptive. Secondly, precisely because all the actions of life are orientated toward the final act of dying, and precisely because the act of dying is the final, irrevocable expression of the meaning of the individual actions of life, the life of Jesus shares in the redemptive significance of his death. Indeed, "... the life and death of Christ in their redemptive significance ... form a unity." [67]

We can see this theory of Rahner's operative in what he has to say about the development of Jesus' consciousness. The most significant exegetical datum with regard to his self-consciousness is, in Rahner's opinion, the gradual realization, in and through the actions of his life and ministry, that he must face death, and that his death itself is an integral part of his mission from the Father. [68]

We may now draw some conclusions from these considerations:

1. It is precisely in the death of Christ that his assumption of a true human nature, like ours except for sin, becomes most evident. The Logos assumed a human nature in its totality and in its individual elements, especially including the ambiguous and terrifying elements which are summarized and symbolized

---

[65] *Ibid.*, p. 69.
[66] *Ibid.*, p. 63.
[67] *Ibid.*, p. 62.
[68] Cf. "The Position of Christology ...," *TI* XI, p. 194.

in human mortality. We can say that Rahner's insistence that in the Incarnation, the Logos assumed human reality as his own and the radically consequential way in which Rahner understands and applies that insight is nothing more — or less — than his attempt to apply the soteriological principle *"Quod non est assumptum, non est sanatum,"* — what has not been assumed, has not been redeemed — to a contemporary understanding of human reality, an understanding in which the ontic, ontological and existential all have their role to play.

2. Rahner's theory of the meaning of death helps us to put our focus on the *death* of Christ as the absolute redemptive event. This is in sharp contrast with the satisfaction theory, which emphasizes the suffering.

3. Rahner's theory of death helps us to appreciate the *mystery* of Christ's death. The unique, redemptive character of Christ's death must be seen in this: not only in that he died, but in that he willingly assumed the experience of death as a consequence of sin, i.e., death as darkness, suffering, fear and trembling, even though he himself was sinless. We find here an echo of Romans 5.

2.2.2.2. Welt (*World*) *as* Mitwelt (*Milieu*): *Cosmic Redemption*

Rahner's understanding of the person of Christ allows him to treat of the cosmic effects of redemption, a topic very much evident in the scriptural data, but practically lacking in traditional textbook soteriology.

We saw above how Rahner has placed the Incarnation in the context of Creation; how his understanding of man in an evolutionary context sees man as the *locus* of the self-realization and further development of the cosmos; and how he understands the meaning of Christ in such a world-view.[69] All of this must be presupposed in our present discussion, and will in turn be clarified by it.

The cosmos is anthropocentric. Ontically, man is the highpoint of material creation, that unique being in whom matter is joined to spirit by giving itself over to spirit to be determined by it. Ontologically, man knows himself to be this unique combination and he experiences the rest of creation as the source of his knowledge of himself and as the goal of the operation of his freedom in which he realizes himself. Existentially, man

---

[69] Cf. *supra*, p. 71f.

experiences the world as his *Mitwelt*, his milieu. In and through
this essential relationship to matter, man is both individuated
from other worldly realities and at the same time related to
them.

In the act of dying there is a separation of body and soul.
Man no longer has the same relationship to the body, and
through that body to the rest of the cosmos, which he had during
life. But because materiality belongs to the essence of man,
we cannot say that he loses this essential determination by becoming acosmic, for the would thereby cease to be man. Nor
can we accept the theory of the transmigration of souls or rein-
carnation, for that would rob man of his historical unicity. Nor
can we postulate some kind of reabsorption into the cosmos,
as if nature continued by "feeding off" those who have died, for
this would deny the immortality of the soul. For all of these
reasons, Rahner postulates a new relationship to matter for the
souls of the dead, a relationship he calls *pancosmic*. Since this
relationship is beyond our experience, he cannot precisely define
it. But it is *essential*, because it is part of the essential constitu-
tion of man, and it is *conceptually* capable of being understood
as the perfection of man's fundamental openness to the world
as such. It is *not* an informing of the cosmos by the soul, *nor*
is it an omnipresence of the soul. It is, however, a real ontological determination of the cosmos.[70]

It is in this context that Rahner attempts to interpret the
cosmic effects of the redemption. In assuming a human nature
the Logos assumes a real part of the cosmos as his own. Because he becomes *man*, he assumes a relationship to the cosmos
which is different from his relationship as God to the cosmos.
It is a relationship in which the world becomes his *Mitwelt*, his
milieu, determining him and in turn being determined by him.[71]

The death of Jesus does not cause this relationship to the
cosmos to cease. Death initiates a pancosmic relationship to
the world in which each man "... in some way introduces as his
contribution the result of his life into the radical, real ground
of the unity of the world." [72] The same is true of Christ. As
Rahner states his position:

> ... through Christ's death, his spiritual reality, which he pos-
> sessed from the beginning, enacted in his life, and brought to

---

[70] Cf. Rahner, "On the Theology of Death," *op. cit.*, pp. 16-26.
[71] Cf. Rahner, "Christology in the Setting ..." *TI* XI, p. 219.
[72] Rahner, "On the Theology of Death," *op. cit.*, p. 63.

consummation in his death, becomes open to the whole world
and is inserted into this whole world in its own ground as a
permanent determination of a real ontological kind.[73]

This is the basis of Rahner's interpretation of Christ's descent
into hell. In his radical unity with mankind because of the
Incarnation, Christ, in death, assumes that very relationship with
the world which is common to all men who have died. Prior to
any consideration of the resurrection, Christ's death has significance for the cosmos. Through his death, Christ makes his own
unique contribution to the real ontological unity of the cosmos,
as do all men. But precisely because the human reality of Christ
is the highest realization of what it means to be man, precisely
because in him the self-communication of God and the absolutely
free acceptance of that communication are hypostatically united,[74]
the perfection and culmination of the universe become real determining factors of the cosmos through his death.[75]

> When the vessel of his body was shattered in death, Christ was
> poured out over all the cosmos; he became actually, in his
> very humanity, what he has always been by his dignity, the
> heart of the universe, the innermost centre of creation.[76]

Thus because of the Hypostatic Union, and apart from the full
revelation of glorified humanity in the resurrection, the death of
Jesus has a redemptive effect on the whole cosmos. The full
implications of this redemption, however, are only revealed to
us in the resurrection.

2.2.2.3. *The Resurrection: The Revelation of Being Redeemed*

Rahner's critique of traditional soteriology's treatment of
the resurrection leads him to attempt to draw out the soteriological significance of this central event of Christian faith. His
starting point is an attempt at a correct understanding of Good

---

[73] *Ibid.*, p. 63. Cf. *idem.*, "The Resurrection of the Body," *TI* II,
p. 210ff; "The Hermeneutics of Eschatological Assertions," *TI* IV, pp. 323-
346; "The Life of the Dead," *TI* IV, pp. 347-354.
    [74] Cf. Rahner, "Christology within an Evolutionary View of the World,"
TI V, p. 174f.
    [75] Rahner, "On the Theology of Death," *op. cit.*, p. 66. For a discussion
of this question and a critique of Rahner's view, cf. J. Strynkowski, *The
Descent of Christ Among the Dead*, unpublished dissertation (Rome: Pontifical Gregorian University, 1971), esp. p. 197ff.
    [76] *Ibid.*, p. 66.

Friday, i.e., of the death of Christ, and of Holy Saturday, i.e., of Christ's descent into hell. We have dealt with his thought on those two salvific events in the previous two sections.

For Rahner, the resurrection of Christ is the manifestation, the revelation of the meaning of Christ's death and descent into hell.[77] The meaning of the resurrection in his view is much more profound than what apologetics has to say about it, and it supersedes the merely personal salvation and blessedness of the humanity of Christ. Precisely because of the Hypostatic Union the resurrection from the dead of the humanity of Christ means the eternal and irrevocable acceptance by God of the reparation for sin which Jesus made through his life and his death. Furthermore, the resurrection means the acceptance of the human nature of Christ as hypostatically joined to the Logos as the permanent condition of the Logos for all eternity. The perdurance of the Incarnation for all eternity is the breakthrough point for the divinization of mankind in eternal blessedness.[78]

Beyond these "personal" meanings of the resurrection for the Logos, this salvific event also has its cosmic effects. The resurrection of Christ is the "final beginning of the glorification and divinization of the whole of reality."[79] Because a part of the this-worldly, material reality has been glorified and divinized and accepted by God for all eternity, the cosmic effects of sin as they penetrated to the very depths of all material reality have been overcome. Because of the real ontological unity of the cosmos, the resurrection of Christ is the revelation and declaration to the cosmos of the absolute future in eschatological victory of God's grace.

For mankind in particular, the resurrection of Christ is the revelation of what it means to be redeemed. The glorified humanity of Christ is, ontologically, the state of definitive salvation.[80] Theologically, on the basis of the exegetical data, it is not the negation of death by a restoration to life as we know it. It is rather a transposition of the life of Jesus onto a different level. It is a level in which the whole meaning of his life, as it was summed up in his death, i.e., the history of Jesus of Nazareth, becomes transhistorical and eternally valid. The tran-

---

[77] Rahner, "Dogmatic Questions on Easter," *TI* IV, p. 127.
[78] *Ibid.*, p. 128f.
[79] *Ibid.*, p. 129.
[80] Rahner, "The Position of Christology ...," *TI* XI, p. 207.

sposition itself is testimony "... to the fact that he has been eternally and definitively saved by God." [81]

This insight of Rahner's provides the ontological and theological ground for what traditional soteriology says about the life and death of Jesus. It is precisely because the resurrection is an act of revelation in which the eschatological victory of Christ is manifested to us that Christ's life and death have meaning for us.

> The message which Jesus utters through his person and through his words can be the unsurpassable and abiding word of God only if the reality that it constitutes (including in this the words that he utters and the fate that he endures) is God's own realiy in the manner which we seek to express by the term "hypostatic union." [82]

It is so, because this has been revealed to us in the resurrection.

This, then, becomes the basis for apologetics. And the fact that the life and death of Jesus have been validated by God in this act of revelation which we call resurrection is precisely the basis of why it is valid to draw moral teaching and example from the events of his life and death. It is the validation of all the claims he made for himself during his life, namely, that he is not just another prophet, but *the* eschatological teacher whose person and message are essentially one.[83] In the resurrection of Christ we have the revelation that God's offer of salvation and its acceptance by man are forever one in Jesus Christ. According to Rahner it is precisely *this* aspect of the resurrection which establishes Jesus for all eternity as the mediator of salvation for all men. It is in the resurrection that we have the revelation of the meaning of Jesus' words: "I am the way, and the truth, and the life; no one comes to the Father, but by me" (Jn 14:6).

The resurrection is, furthermore, the basis of cult. The transposition of the life and sacrificial death of Christ which occurs in the resurrection posits them into an eternity of ontological reality. This is not merely a pancosmic relationship. It is not merely the "living on" of some dead person's good deeds and accomplishments as real ontological factors in the cosmos. Precisely because the deeds and accomplishments of

---

[81] *Ibid.*, p. 208.
[82] *Ibid.*, p. 205.
[83] *Ibid.*, p. 201ff.

Jesus of Nazareth have been eternally assumed by God, via the perdurance of the Hypostatic Union, into the innertrinitarian Being of God himself, they have become a real ontological condition of God's relationship to the world and of mankind's relationship to God. It is this factor which grounds the true *anamnesis* which is the basis of Christian worship.[84]

In summary we may say that the resurrection of Christ has a soteriological significance of its own. According to Rahner, the resurrection "... is the very reality of the soteriological significance of his [Jesus'] temporal life, accepted by God, set free to work, and actually effective." [85]

2.2.3.0. MEDIATION

The foregoing considerations of Rahner's soteriology have brought us to the point where we can discuss his thought on the mediation of Christ in more detail.

2.2.3.1. *Intercommunication as the Ontological Basis of Mediation*

Rahner begins his thought on the mediation of Christ by asking the question: « ... what is the transcendental horizon of understanding, and thus the hermeneutical principle, which will lead to an understanding of the mediatorship of Christ which can be protected from misconceptions?" [86] In other words, Rahner says that the concept of mediated salvation is by no means a concept that we can take for granted. That salvation is an act of God alone, that he alone can overcome man's sinfulness, is not surprising. That this act should be accomplished in Jesus of Nazareth, who was one with us in humanity, and that this accomplishment of salvation should be valid for all time, even for the time *before* the history of Jesus of Nazareth, are concepts which must seek out their ontological basis, according to Rahner, if they are not to be misunderstood and given a mythological, unhistorical interpretation.[87]

Rahner seeks the ontological basis of mediation in the radically intercommunicative character of human existence.[88]

---

84 Rahner, "Dogmatic Questions on Easter," *TI* IV, p. 129ff.
85 *Ibid.*, p. 131.
86 Rahner, "One Mediator and Many Mediations," *TI* IX, p. 175.
87 *Ibid.*, p. 175.
88 *Ibid.*, p. 176.

We could use terms such as "solidarity" and "sociability" to describe what Rahner means by intercommunication. Human existence is intercommunicative existence, and this intercommunication is experienced by man and is exhibited in the world in a variety of ways. Rahner enumerates a few of them: "... the physical unity of the cosmos, the space-time unity; biological unity; intercommunication in the unity of a single history of truth and love, untruth and hate; the unity of rootedness in God, etc." [89]

This intercommunication is so radical that there simply is no completely private sphere to which man can withdraw and be separated from his relationships to others. What happens to others necessarily affects us, even if it only reminds us of the fate of mankind which we all share. On a moral level we experience this intercommunication as a solidarity in good and evil, in the personal and social experience of love of neighbor and of sin. [90] And because it is such a radical characteristic of man's being human, it is also a factor in his search for salvation.

> If, therefore, the question of salvation is an unavoidable element of human existence, intercommunication is also a factor of existence, whether for or against salvation. Here too no-one is alone; each one supports every other person, in the matter of salvation everyone is responsible and sginificant for everyone else. [91]

Moreover, according to Rahner, intercommunication is an essential element in man's relationship to God. It is one of those elements of human experience in which man can come naturally to a knowledge of God. Man's experience of his radical unity and solidarity with all other men and with the entire cosmos is one experience, which when reflected upon by the light of reason, can lead to a certain knowledge of the existence of God. [92] From all of these considerations we can see that the intercommunicative nature of man is one of those essential characteristics of man that dispose him to be the addressee of revelation. Because the world speaks to man of his intercommunicative existence and because man experiences and recognizes this

---

89 *Ibid.*, p. 179.
90 *Ibid.*, p. 177.
91 *Ibid.*, p. 176.
92 *Ibid.*, p. 177.

existence within himself, God himself can establish intercommunication with man via the self-communication of his grace.[93]

Theologically, throughout salvation history, human intercommunication has been a constitutive element of God's action
among men. Concepts such as "People of God" and "Covenant"
make this clear.[94] This reaches its high point in the Incarnation, for in this event we have at one and the same time the
absolute self-communication of God and its absolute free acceptance by a man. If we understand the Hypostatic Union
properly as the assumption of a true, full human nature by the
Logos, then intercommunication is necessarily an element in the
Incarnation. Because Jesus is truly man, truly a part of this
cosmos, he has a relationship of intercommunicative solidarity
with all men and with the cosmos. This, then, is the ontological
basis for his unique mediatorship.

2.2.3.2. *The Humanity of Christ as Instrumental Cause of Mediation*

If the humanity of Jesus is the ontological basis of his solidarity with us, and hence of his ability to mediate for us from
our side, the perdurance of the humanity of Christ, i.e., its eternal
and final acceptance by God as part of his own reality, is the
basis of Christ's mediation from the side of God. Rahner points
out that, if the glorified humanity of Christ is to be more than
some kind of museum piece in heaven, more than a reality whose
importance and meaning lies solely in the past because it was
at one time instrumental in saving mankind, then the present
function of that humanity, hypostatically united to the Logos,
must be reflected upon and brought home in soteriology.[95]

Rahner sees a point of departure for such a development
in the theological teaching of the necessity of the *lumen gloriae*
as a mediation to the immediacy of the beatific vision. This
lumen gloriae is itself created grace because it is an elevating
effect created in the soul of man by means of which he has
access to the immediate vision of God as the culmination of the
uncreated grace of the divine indwelling.[96] Rahner interprets
the cause of this *lumen gloriae* to be the glorified humanity of

---

[93] *Ibid.*, p. 178.   Cf. *DS* 3004, 3026.
[94] *Ibid.*, p. 178.
[95] Rahner, "Current Problems in Christology," *TI* I, p. 192ff.
[96] Cf. Rahner and Vorgrimmler, "Anschauung Gottes," *Kleines Theologisches Wörterbuch, op. cit.,* p. 22f.

Christ. As such the glorified humanity of Christ is the instrumental cause of the beatific vision itself.[97] Thus the humanity of Christ has a continuing, eternal mediating function.

The arrival at this point completes the summary of the structural elements of Rahner's Christology which has been the concern of this chapter. We can say that all of Rahner's thought is fundamentally incarnational, beginning with the creation and ending with eschatology. The humanity of Christ as hypostatically united to the Logos is at one and the same time:

1) the full revelation of these mysteries in themselves because it is the revelation of the supreme mystery of God himself;

2) the unique human appropriation of these mysteries with regard to Jesus himself;

3) the means by which all men come to know and appropriate these mysteries in the salvific process which is God's will for all men.

Rahner's Christology is the key to understanding all of his diverse theological writings, for if there is any one thread which runs through his work it is precisely this: that the humanity of Christ is both the starting point and the hermeneutical principle of all theology.

For this humanity is what God becomes when God expresses himself in that which is "other" than himself. On the basis of this definition, the humanity of Christ is the key systematic link in theology. Christ's humanity defines our humanity — it is the key to anthropology; Christ's humanity is the self-impartation of the trinitarian God — it is the key to the doctrine of God; Christ's humanity in its communion with the Father discloses the ultimate goal of human life — it is the key to eschatology; Christ's humanity as the *Realsymbol* of the Logos exemplifies the sacramental essence of the church and the meaning of the sacraments — it is the key to ecclesiology; Christ's humanity means the divinization of man and the forgiveness of sins — it is the key to soteriology; Christ's humanity as the self-expression of God in uncreated grace defines the

---

[97] Cf. Rahner, "The Eternal Significance ...," *TI* III, p. 44f., and *idem*, "Dogmatic Questions on Easter," *TI* IV, p. 131f. Rahner himself never works out completely this theological opinion. For a good theological foundation of this opinion cf. J. Alfaro, "Cristo Glorioso, Revelador del Padre," *Gregorianum* 39 (1958), 222-270, especially 257ff.

horizon of general revelation ontologically and noetically — it
is the key to the problem of nature and grace.[98]

The humanity of Christ is eternally the means by which God
comes to us in revelation and grace. The humanity of Christ
is eternally the means by which we go to God in knowledge
and love. In light of this we may now seek to verify the symbol
of the Heart of Christ as Rahner has proposed it to us by showing the relationships which exist between his Christology and
his writings on the Devotion to the Sacred Heart.

---

[98] W. Shepherd, *Man's Condition* (New York: Herder and Herder, 1969),
p. 178f.

CHAPTER III

THE VERIFICATION OF THE RAHNERIAN INTERPRETATION OF THE SYMBOL OF THE HEART OF CHRIST IN TERMS OF HIS CHRISTOLOGY

3.0. INTRODUCTION

The purpose of this chapter is to verify Rahner's usage of the symbol of the Heart of Christ in terms of the Christological synthesis of Chapter II. By "verify," we mean that we will try to draw out the relationships which exist between Rahner's theology of the Devotion to the Sacred Heart and his Christology. If Rahner has offered some unique insights into the Devotion itself, it is our belief that those insights arise from his own Christological synthesis. Implicit in this verification process are some concrete examples of the relationship of theology and spirituality. These implications will be made explicit in our concluding chapter.

The methodology we will follow will be to treat the sections of Chapter II as they relate specifically to the Rahnerian exposition of the Devotion to the Sacred Heart. We will treat them in reverse order.[1] There will be a certain overlapping with the end of Chapter I.[2] However, this will not be repetitious, since the results will be more developed. In the second section of this chapter we will briefly deal with Rahner's attempt to develop a Christology "from below" and its implications for the symbol of the Heart of Christ.

3.1.0. THE HEART OF CHRIST AND SOTERIOLOGY

In our discussion of the use of the symbol of the Heart in the Devotion, we discovered that the symbol presents us with

---

[1] By reversing the order we will proceed from the foundation of the symbol to an interpretation of its meaning, as will be seen in the exposition itself.

[2] Cf. *supra*, pp. 48ff.

a two-fold movement, an inward movement in which the personal
center of Christ is revealed in the symbol, and an outward movement, itself a double movement, from God to man in revelation and from man to God in atonement. We will now undertake
the verification of each of these movements by relating them to
the foregoing Christological synthesis.

3.1.1.0. *The Perduring Humanity of Christ as the Basis of the Symbol, Hence of the Devotion*

Traditionally, the object of the Devotion to the Sacred Heart
has been interpreted as having some intrinsic connection with
the physical heart of the glorified humanity of Christ. But because of the lack of an adequate understanding of symbolism,
this theology of the Devotion had difficulty deciding exactly what
constituted the proper object of the Devotion.[3] However, we
can discern here the basic theological reason for offering *latria*
to the humanity of Christ. *Latria* is possible precisely because
the humanity of Christ perdures in the eternity of the Hypostatic
Union. One of the difficulties of this traditional theology of the
Devotion lies in the fact that its Christological underpinnings
lacked a developed understanding of the *present* active role of
the humanity of Christ in the work of redeeming us in the here
and now. Thus much of the discussion of the Heart of Christ
centered on its past meaning in the life of the historical Jesus,
especially the suffering of the Lord during his passion.

The perdurance of the humanity of Christ and its active
role in the work of redemption *now* play a much larger role in
Rahner's theology of the Devotion. Indeed, that perdurance is
essential if Rahner's theory of symbolism is to be able to operate.
Because the humanity of Christ lives in all eternity, his human
heart is the real symbol of his unique personal center, and it
is this not simply in a backward looking contemplation of what
at one time was the importance of that heart as the symbol of
the redemptive love from which Christ's saving actions sprang.
Rather the symbol makes present the Christ who lives now
forever, who continues to redeem us by his love.

This formal viewpoint is reflected in what Rahner has to
say about the practice of consoling the Lord in the contemplation of the passion. Because the symbol of the Heart of Christ
makes present to us the Lord as he is now, i.e., as he who in

---

[3] Cf. Gutzwiller, "The Opposition," in Stierli, *op. cit.*, p. 1ff.

his glory bears the marks of his suffering on the cross, the symbol, therefore presents us with Christ under the totality of his saving work on our behalf.[4] As we have seen in Rahner's soteriology, the mediating role of Christ is past in the life and death, present in the resurrection and grace, and eternally future in the mediation to beatific vision. Each of these phases of his one mediatorship takes place in and through his humanity. Thus the perdurance of the humanity of Christ, as Rahner has interpreted it, is precisely the reason why the symbol can function at all.

3.1.1.1. *Intercommunication and the Symbol of the Heart*

If the perdurance of the humanity of Christ is the basis for the functioning of the symbol, the intercommunicative nature of human reality which was the basis of Christ's mediative relationship to us is the reason why the Heart of Christ is an *Ursymbol*. We must recall that primordial symbolism consists precisely in the fact of making a being present in its original unity primarily for itself and secondarily for others.[5] The heart is the "dynamic ground out of which man seeks his most original and never adequately obtainable self-understanding and in which alone he can find it."[6] Thus the heart is the primary, primordial symbol of the unique Hypostatic Unity of Jesus *for Jesus himself*. It is also the symbol of his unique unity *for us*, and the ultimate ground for this communication of his meaning to us must be sought in the intercommunicative relationship which he has with us because of the Hypostatic Union.

We can find meaning in the Heart of Jesus precisely because each of us searches for our own meaning in this same symbol. Intercommunication in this context means that each man seeks the original unity of his existence in searching for his heart and expresses what he has found there by his attitudes and actions toward others and the world. There is solidarity in the searching, and there is solidarity in the effects of this "cordial" self-expression in the world. Jesus' solidarity with us because of the Hypostatic Union means that he, too, had to

---

[4] Cf. *supra*, p. 59f.

[5] Cf. *supra*, p. 24.

[6] K. Rahner and H. Vorgrimmler, "Herz," *K th W*, p. 170. German text: "der dynamische Grund, von dem aus er sein ureigenstes u. niemals adäquat einholbares Selbstverständnis sucht u. in dem allein er es finden kann."

search for his heart, for the original unity of his being, and we can appreciate this search in terms of Rahner's interpretation of the problem of the knowledge and self-consciousness of Christ.[7] What the Lord discovers in the search for his heart is his divine Sonship, his mission from the Father, his vocation to die in obedience on the cross for the sins of men. What the Lord expresses to the world as the result of this discovery of his heart is the incarnate love of God, a love that expresses itself in the world precisely in and through his humanity.

Intercommunication, then, provides the ground for the communication of meaning through the symbol. And this intercommunication itself has its ground in the fact of the Hypostatic Union. Because he is one with us in humanity, the Heart of Christ can mediate to us the meaning of his actions in the world in which we come to know who he is in himself. This meaning is communicated to us because in order to know ourselves, we must go out of our selves in an encounter with what is other. When we return to ourselves in light of the encounter with the Heart of Christ, we return with the meaning which was mediated to us by the symbol of the Heart.

Thus the humanity of Christ in its glorified state is the very foundation of the symbolism of his Heart. Because his humanity perdures, his Heart can be a real symbol for us; and because of his intercommunicative relationship with us (based on the reality of his human nature), Christ's Heart discloses his personal meaning to us. We will now treat of what is disclosed in the symbol in light of Rahner's Christology.

3.1.2.0. THE HEART OF CHRIST AND THE RESURRECTION

In Chapter II we saw how Rahner develops the meaning of the resurrection in terms of his Christology. The resurrection of Christ establishes the identity of the historical Jesus and the risen Lord. It is the event which links the humanity of Jesus of Nazareth and the glorified humanity of the Lord. As such it is the supreme event of revelation.

In the previous two sections we have seen the consequences of this for the functioning of the Heart as a real symbol. It is precisely this identity which is established by the resurrection which enables us to say that the symbol we are speaking of is

---

[7] Cf. *supra*, p. 76ff.

the physical heart of the glorified Christ which bears within it the marks of his passion and death.

We also saw that the resurrection of Christ, as an event of revelation, provides the basis for *anamnesis*, for considering the events of the life of Christ as a moral model for Christian life, for our relationship to the world, and for our relationship as men with God.[8] We will now consider each of these factors individually in their relationship with the symbol of the Heart of Christ and the Devotion itself.

3.1.2.1. *The Heart of Christ and Anamnesis*

In Rahner's theory of symbolism, the symbol functions as a mediation to direct presence of the symbolized. Because the humanity of Christ has achieved a transhistorical relationship to the world as a result of the resurrection, the symbol of his Heart makes Christ present to us in that transhistorical relationship. Thus the Heart of Christ as a real symbol of his relationship to us incorporates all the elements of his past, present and future relationships to the work of our salvation. In this way the Heart of Christ presents us with the whole mystery of Christ in his soteriological mediation on our behalf. It is the Heart of him who by his life, death and resurrection atoned for our sins; it is the Heart of him who at the present time mediates all graces to us; it is the Heart of him who mediates the direct vision of God in eternal blessedness.[9]

Because of this transhistorical mediation by the symbol of the Heart we can say that the Heart of Christ places us in a basic relationship of *anamnesis* with the saving work of Christ.[10]

---

[8] Cf. *supra* p. 89ff.

[9] This instrumental causality of the humanity of Christ in the mediation of grace is one of the reasons why all grace is *gratia Christi*. According to Rahner, traditional theology makes this presupposition without working it out. Cf. "The Theology of the Symbol," *TI* IV, p. 241ff., and "Current Problems in Christology," *TI*, p. 199.

[10] We use *anamnesis* in this context in an analogous sense. Anamnesis in a proper sense refers to the ritual reenactment of a past event in the present, thereby making that event ritually present and positing it as having future validity. This ritual anamnesis is properly celebrated in a community context. Cf. J.-J. von Allmen, *Worship: Its Theology and Practice* (London: Lutterworth Press, 1965), 32ff.; M. Thurian, *The Eucharistic Memorial*, Part 1: The Old Testament (London: Lutterworth Press, 1960), and Part 2: The New Testament (London: Lutterworth Press, 1961), *passim*; S. Marsili, *Teologia Liturgica*, vol. II: La Messa, Mistero

Through this relation with his saving meaning for us we come to a relationship with his person. We use the word *anamnesis* to describe this relationship because it is more than just a simple remembering through the agency of the symbol of the Heart. If it were a simple remembering, the symbol would be reduced to a sign, a convention that reminds us of something else. Rahner's theory of symbolism as it is applied to the Heart of Christ requires the notion of *presence* of the symbolized in a real relationship which is mediated by the symbol. For Rahner, that presence which man experiences in the act of knowing and loving is sufficient to fulfill this requirement.[11]   Hence we can predicate an *anamnetic presence* of the work and person of Christ, mediated to us through the symbol of his Heart, without confusing this kind of presence with the properly sacramental presence of the Church's liturgy.

This anamnetic presence through the symbol establishes the foundation of the cultic relationship of *latria* to the Heart of Christ. It is the essential relationship between the symbol and the thing symbolized which lies at the basis of this fact. Precisely because the symbol makes the symbolized present, our relationship in knowledge and love is mediated by the symbol to the thing symbolized. Thus because the symbol of the Heart makes Christ present to us in his person and his work on our behalf, in adoring the symbol we really are adoring Christ himself. It is precisely here that we see the importance of the ontological connection which Rahner posits between the real symbol and the thing symbolized. Without such an understanding of the intrinsic relationship between a being and its real symbol, much of the Church's liturgical and devotional life would be in danger of grave misunderstanding.

In our opinion, we can see in the anamnetic presence of Christ in the symbol of the Heart part of the reason for the "natural" opening of the Devotion to the Sacred Heart to a

---

Pasquale del N. T. (Rome: Pont. Ateneo S. Anselmo, 1973), p. 73ff. *Ad usum Privatum.*

Our usage of anamnesis is *analogous* because the ritual and public elements of Devotion to the Heart of Christ lack the necessary sacramental elements of true liturgical anamnesis. All the other elements are present, however. It would be an interesting question for spirituality to investigate to what extent every relationship to Christ bears this basic anamnetic characteristic, but such an investigation is obviously beyond the scope of this thesis.

[11] Cf. *supra*, p. 28ff.

eucharistic expression.   Precisely because the Eucharist is the
anamnetic presence of Christ *par excellence*, with all the objective efficacy implied in the Church's teaching on *opus operatum*
in the sacraments, there is a natural, dynamic connection between the two symbols.   We see evidence of this connection
both in the Paray form of the Devotion, with its communion of
reparation and the practice of the Holy Hour, and in later developments in the Devotion, such as the Devotion to the Eucharistic Heart of Jesus.

3.1.2.2. *The Heart of Christ and Love*

Because the symbol of the Heart of Christ makes his soteriological meaning present to us in its totality, we can find in the
symbol the revelation of the Love of God for us.   The unified
summary of meaning which is mediated to us by the symbol
of the Heart of Christ is precisely that three-fold love which
has been traditional in the theology of the Devotion.[12]   Jesus
Christ is in his humanity the revelation of the Logos through
whom we come to know the Trinity whose essence is Love.   In
his humanity, too, Christ reveals what it means to be graced
with the infused divine love of God himself.   Jesus Christ, in
the reality of his human nature, is one with us in the experience
of true, human affection and emotion.   In the actions which flow
from this three-fold love, which is a reality present in the world
by means of the mediation of his humanity, Jesus reveals himself as the real symbol of God's redemptive love for man.

In our discussion of Rahner's theory of symbolism, we saw
that one of the characteristics of a real symbol is that in communicating its meaning to us, it evokes a response.[13]   As a result,
the Heart of Christ, as the real symbol of his loving person,
must evoke a proper response in communicating Christ to us.
In fact, one of the elements of the Devotion is precisely the
return of love for the love of Christ.   This expresses itself both
in reparation and in apostolic action.

Furthermore, the symbol itself discloses the kind of response
of love which is proper to its conveyed meaning.   The return
of love is not some kind of vague, moral imperative, nor can
it be achieved in a kind of quietism.   The revelation of love
which the symbol makes present to us is precisely an incarnate,
active love.

---

[12] Cf. *supra*, p. 55.
[13] Cf. *supra*, p. 40f.

For this reason, then, the proper response demanded by the symbol itself is an active love which incarnates itself in this world. The love we return to God for his loving actions on our behalf is a love which expresses itself in action in this world. Thus there is a unity between the Christian's love of God and his love of neighbor, and this unity has its basis precisely in the Incarnation itself.[14] This unity is essentially communicated in the symbol of the Heart of Christ itself. It is precisely in the Heart of Christ, his physical, human heart, that we find the source of his loving action in the world. Those actions *are in themselves* the revelation of God's love for us.[15] Thus the symbol of the Sacred Heart, by making Christ present to us under the aspect of his loving action on our behalf, both conveys the meaning of Christ to us and dictates the proper response which we must give in light of that revelation.

3.1.2.3. *The Heart of Christ as Symbol of Redemption*

We saw in Chapter II that the resurrection of Christ is the revelation of the final state of redemption.[16] The acceptance of the humanity of Christ into the reality of God for all eternity is the revelation of God's unconditioned redemptive love for the world. The perdurance of the humanity of Jesus establishes a real ontological condition of God's relationship to the world, and the world's relationship to God.

Inasmuch as the Heart of Christ, as a real symbol, makes Christ present to us in his redemptive relationship to us and God, it is also a symbol of the redemption of the world. As such, it conveys to us the proper mode of the Christian's relationship to the world, and to God.

For Rahner, this relationship, which is conveyed by the symbol, has its effects for man's religious experience. Our relationship to God has its origin in God, is borne along by the power of God's grace, and has its fulfillment in God himself. But this does not mean that we find God to the degree that we estrange ourselves from the world. The very fact that the symbol of this relationship is a physical part of this world which has been

---

[14] Cf. K. Rahner, "The 'Commandment' of Love in Relation to the Other Commandments," *TI* V, p. 439ff., and *idem*, "Reflections on the Unity of the Love of Neighbour and the Love of God," *TI* VI, p. 231ff.

[15] Cf. *supra*, p. 45f.

[16] Cf. *supra*, p. 89ff.

assumed by God as his own reality gives the lie to this basically unchristian way of thinking.

For Rahner, man's relationship to God, viewed as the appropriation of redemption, involves a three-fold movement.[17] The first is leaving the creature to find God. This relationship may be identified with man's fundamental self-transcendence. In and through his relationship to the world, man comes to a relationship to God as the Absolute. For the Christian, this relationship is with the God who has revealed himself in Jesus Christ as Love. The second movement is from God to the creature. In this second movement we proceed from God to the world in imitation of God's own relationship to the world which is eternally symbolized in the Incarnation. This movement involves us in loving the world as God has loved it. The third movement, the highest mode of our relationship to God, is finding the created reality of this world in God. This is not a pantheistic relationship to God as the *esse omnium*, the only real being that exists. It is, rather, the appropriation of the fact that the creature exists as the creative self-expression of God. God has revealed himself as Love by creating the other in which he can express himself. In the created humanity of Jesus we find the ultimate expression of this divine essence, because the Hypostatic Union means precisely the creation of an "other" capable of expressing that love, i.e., a human nature, and at the same time the acceptance for all eternity of that "other" as God's own reality. This provides the sense of Rahner's statement, "... if God is love, one comes closest to it [i.e., the divine Love] where, having given itself as love to the world, it is furthest away from itself."[18]

Because this relationship is expressed in the humanity of Jesus himself, and symbolized for us in the Sacred Heart, we can say that the symbol of the Heart of Christ conveys to the Christian the paradigm of his relationship to the world. The world does not disappear in the Christian's religious acts. It is "not *maya*, the veil, which dissolves like mist before the sun the more one recognizes the Absolute, i.e., the more religious one becomes."[19] Rather, the world is precisely the *redeemed* world, the world which God loves unconditionally. We can find our salvation in this world precisely because it has been loved

---

[17] Rahner, "The Eternal Significance ...," *TI* III, p. 40ff.
[18] *Ibid.*, p. 43.
[19] *Ibid.*, p. 40.

unconditionally by God. This has been revealed to us in the
humanity of Christ, and as such it must be a part of any true
devotion to the humanity of Christ. It is precisely this perspective of Rahner's Christology which is the basis of his rejection
of all false quietism which may have been associated with the
Devotion to the Sacred Heart in the past.

3.1.2.4. *The Heart of Crist and Christian Anthropology*

In Chapter II we saw the relationship between Rahner's
Christology and his theological anthropology.[20] In Rahner's
thought, Jesus Christ is the fulfillment of all of man's existential possibilities. Jesus is at one and the same time man's openness to God and the acceptance of that openness as God's own
reality. The effects of this Hypostatic Union on the human
nature of Christ are basically the same as the effects of the divine
indwelling in grace on all men.

In this sense Jesus is the high point, the insurpassable example, of what happens to man in the encounter with God in
revelation and grace. And precisely because this is the fulfillment of that existential potentiality which is identical with
human essence, we can say that Jesus is in his humanity the
perfect example of what it means to be man.

But this exemplary nature of Jesus is more than simply an
ethical ideal. Because his humanity is the reality of God, it
is endowed with a power which goes beyond merely admiring
the ethical goodness which is portrayed in the actions of his
life and death. The humanity of Christ is the mediating means
by which we are graced with the power of God not only to become like Christ in our actions, but to become "other Christs"
in a real, ontological sense.

For this reason we can say that the humanity of Christ is
the axiological factor in a Christian understanding of man. The
value of Christian life is measured precisely to the extent that
the Christian appropriates the whole complex of meaning which
is presented to him in the humanity of Christ. To the extent
that the symbol of the Heart of Jesus presents Christ to us in
the perfection of his humanity through grace, a perfection manifested in the saving actions which sprang from his loving union
with the Logos in the Hypostatic Union, to that extent the symbol of his Heart has this axiological quality to it. Here again

---

[20] Cf. *supra*, p. 67ff.

we see the symbol functioning both in terms of communicating meaning to us and in eliciting a proper response from us.

In terms of a Christian anthropology, we can say that the symbol of the Heart of Christ presents us with three basic elements of a theological anthropology such as Rahner has developed. First, the Heart of Christ symbolizes the basic relationship of man to God. Man finds the perfection of his nature in the realization of that obediential potentiality which he is by his very nature. This is present in the symbol to the extent that the symbol incorporates Christ's free surrender in obedience to the will of his Father. In the person of Jesus we have the revelation though his life, death and resurrection that the highest possibilities of human existence are realized in the perfection which only love of God and loving service of our neighbor can bring about

Second, the Heart of Christ symbolizes the basic incarnational structure of all Christian understanding of man and his relationship to God and the world. The Heart of Christ is a symbol of the permanence of the Incarnation. As such it presents man with a horizon of understanding for all reality. The Heart of Jesus, by pointing to the Incarnation of the Logos, also points to the incarnational structure of grace in Christian life.

Third, the symbol of the Heart of Jesus presents man with his basic eschatological orientation. Because the symbol is the Heart of the glorified Lord, it points toward that fulfillment of the life of grace which can only be achieved in the beatific vision.

In our opinion, the relationship between the Devotion to the Sacred Heart and a Christian anthropology can be seen in such devotional prayers as "Sacred Heart of Jesus, make our hearts like unto Thine." This prayer incorporates both the notion of the exemplary nature of the humanity of Christ and invokes Christ as the mediator who makes this conformity possible by his grace. This kind of relationship, however, can only become explicit in a theology of the Sacred Heart Devotion if the relationship between Christology and anthropology is an operative one, as it is in Rahner.

3.1.2.5. *Summary*

In this section we have seen how the symbol of the Heart of Jesus functions as a unifying factor. Because it is a real primordial symbol, the Heart of Christ is capable of presenting the diversity of the mystery of Christ in a unified way by presenting us with the original unity of Christ himself. That original unity is mediated to us by his Heart, i.e., the symbol of his original center from which all his actions flow and in which that diversity returns to find the unity. In all of this it has been the resurrection of Jesus which has made the real symbol possible, and which is the key link to understanding the meaning that symbol mediates to us.

This whole discussion has taken place in the framework of a transcendental Christology. Within that framework we have seen that the symbol of the Heart of Christ, while not identical with Christianity, is capable of presenting in an existential way what that transcendental Christology presented in an abstract, theoretical manner.

In the Section Two of this chapter we will deal with the question of whether, or how, this symbol is viable in a different Christological context, namely, that of a Christology "from below." We shall discuss Rahner's own attempt to arrive at this kind of Christology and make some observations on the different kind of relationship which exists between the two kinds of Christology and the symbol of the Heart of Christ.

Before we proceed to that discussion, however, and as a way of closing the present discussion, we will deal with Rahner's analysis of his own transcendental Christology and relate this general analysis to the Devotion to the Heart of Christ. This discussion will show how a devotion, such as the Sacred Heart Devotion, relates to a transcendental Christology in general. We have already seen some of the particulars of how the symbol of the Heart of Christ relates to the individual elements of this kind of Christology. This more general reflection on the relationship will help us to see it in a broader sense.

3.1.3.0. RAHNER'S ANALYSIS OF THE STRUCTURE OF TRANSCENDENTAL CHRISTOLOGY

Rahner's structural analysis of transcendental Christology comprises Theses Eight through Fourteen of his attempt to develop a Christology "from below." [21] In this analysis he presents the necessity, the presuppositions, the starting point, the procedure and the task of a transcendental Christology. In this

---

[21] Cf. K. Rahner and W. Thüsing, *Christologie — systematisch und exegetisch* (Freiburg: Herder, 1972), pp. 20-24. *Quaestiones Disputatae* 55.

section we will briefly present what he has to say under each of those headings.

Necessity - The necessity of a transcendental Christology is not resolved by the objections to it, namely, that it cannot of itself ground a concrete relationship with Christ and that it is made possible only by a transcendental anthropology. It is necessary in terms of traditional Christology because traditional Christology does not contain within itself the criteria for judging itself in terms of whether it is mere mythological repetition or of whether those statements which it passes on actually do communicate the faith.[22]

Presuppositions - Transcendental Christology presupposes that in human existence there is a mutual relationship of conditioning between the transcendentally necessary and the historically contingent. This means that these two elements of human existence a) always appear together, b) ground existence itself, c) are of such a unity that one element cannot be reduced to the other, and d) are historically open both as regards the past and the future.[23]

Starting Point - The starting point of transcendental Christology is those human experiences which man inevitably has and none of which can fulfill the demand of absoluteness which he inevitably makes of them. This point of departure includes the relationship between theology and Christology because those experiences are the *locus* of the experience of what man means by God.[24]

Procedure - Transcendental Christology proceeds via a transcendental anthropology to arrive at transcendentally deduced statements about a Saviour. This procedure takes place in five steps:

1) Anthropology understands man as the being of transcendental necessity, which means that in his every encounter with the categorical, man always transcends the categorical to be confronted by the absolute mystery which he calls God.

2) This understanding of man includes his hope that this absolute mystery will not remain as the goal of his striving in an unending movement, but will become the one who gives himself as the fulfillment of the meaning of existence.

3) Because of the unity of the transcendental and the historical in human existence, such a self-revelation of God must be

---

[22] *Ibid.*, Theses 8 and 9, p. 20.
[23] *Ibid.*, Theses 10 and 11, p. 20f.
[24] *Ibid.*, Thesis 12, p. 21.

mediated historically, in categorical consciousness, and hence in time and space; the modality of this self-revelation remains open, but whatever modality emerges from this consideration, God must remain a revealing Self and not become a categorical object.

4) Man's hope for a self-revelation of God looks for *that* event in which God's self-pledging to man is unambivalent and irreversible, hence eschatological; this event may be conceived *either* as the fulfillment itself *or*, considering the continuation of history, as that event in history by which the promise itself is made irreversible without removing its promissory character by a simple, world-wide fulfillment.

5) The categoriality of the event by which this self-promising of God and the hope commensurate to it are historically present can only be a man; this man must be one who gives up any false promise of an innerworldly future by dying, and who in his death shows himself to be the one definitively accepted by God; such a man is what is meant by the absolute Saviour.[25]

Task - The task of transcendental Christology is to reflect upon and articulate man's hope and search for such an absolute Saviour; the historical realization of this Saviour in Jesus of Nazareth lies beyond its scope and is experienced by man in his experience of history itself.[26]

3.1.3.1. *Observations*

Rahner's analysis of a transcendental Christology has its various aspects borne out in the presentation of his Christology which we saw in Chapter II.[27]   In our opinion what lies at the basis of this structural analysis is the distinction between theology and faith, between theory and practice. Faith, as the existential experience of Jesus Christ, as the "practice" of a living-loving relationship to him, and through him to the Triune God, has primacy in this distinction. It is precisely the experience of faith which is the motive for the kind of reflection which is the task of theology. The test of the adequacy of theological reflection must include the adequacy of its reflection on that faith experience.

---

[25] *Ibid.*, Thesis 13, p. 21ff.
[26] *Ibid.*, Thesis 14, p. 24.
[27] We have chosen to present this analysis in the present context because it adds to the discussion of this chapter, namely, the relationship between the symbol of the Heart of Christ and Christology in a Rahnerian framework.

This distinction is formally operative in Rahner's Christology. That Christology is existential in the sense that it begins with the actual experience of Christ both in Christian living and in Christian proclamation, and much of Rahner's critique of traditional school Christology is based on the gulf between that theological reflection and the actually lived Christian experience. It is also operative in the sense that Rahner has tried to be consciously aware of that distinction in the process of developing his own Christology.

> But it [dogmatic reflection and formulation] is such that even then it can only really be understood by us when we make real to ourselves in our faith what he is for us, and what has taken place through him and in him in that saving history which is our own. We must understand that a dogmatic formulation, however much it is, and continues to be, binding upon us, is not something which simply has to be defined in order that everything may be "clear." We must recognize that in the case of any dogmatic formula, in order to really understand it and make it real to ourselves in our faith, we must think back to that in which it properly originated as well.[28]

No theoretical, dogmatic formulation can ever completely and adequately express what the Christian experiences in his faith-relationship with Jesus. Both a metaphysical and a transcendental Christology must be formally aware of this fact both in beginning and in concluding their proper task.

Rahner claims that such an opening of theological reflection back into the level of experience is entirely to be expected. The lack of that kind of opening in traditional school theology is, in his opinion, very evident in the way the Devotion to the Heart of Christ was presented in most manuals of Christology. And the fact that this distinction between theology and faith was not operative in many of those manuals is evident in what Rahner calls "the implicit criticism" of the ends and practice of the Devotion to the Heart of Jesus which is contained in those manuals.[29] Without denying or downplaying any of the difficulties in Rahner's own position, we can say that at least he has formally recognized the inability of theological speculation to fully and adequately express the content of the Christian faith experience.

---

[28] Rahner, "The Position of Christology ...," *TI* XI, p. 204.
[29] Interview with Karl Rahner, December 21, 1975.

A transcendental Christology has for its formal point of view the deduction of the conditions of the possibility of predicating of Jesus the idea of the Saviour. Its *a posteriori* element is the history of Jesus of Nazareth and the faith in him which has been the core of the proclamation of the Church. Its *a priori* element is precisely those experiences which man has which lead him to look for such a thing as a Saviour.[30] The deduction of the conditions of the possibility of a Saviour, however, is not adequate in itself without the return to the experienced reality of Christ. That return might be accompanied by new and deeper insights, and even corrective principles, for that lived experience. In this sense, theology has a critical function to play in relation to the experience, and especially to the forms by which man expresses that experience.

3.1.3.2. *The Role of the Devotion in Relation to Rahner's Transcendental Christology*

In our opinion, the Devotion to the Sacred Heart is one possible way for this return to the reality of the experience of Christ to take place, and it functions this way in terms of Rahner's transcendental Christology. If the experience of Jesus which is prior to a transcendental analysis is a unified experience, and if a transcendental analysis involves man in the diverse elements which are the constituent parts of that unity, then man needs some way in which he can reunite those elements and find them again in their primordial unity. It is in this sense that the symbol of the Heart can function as a bridge back to the primordial unity of the experience of Jesus in the life of the Christian.

The transcendental analysis necessarily isolates the individual elements of the unified experience. This enables it to return to the unity of the experience of Christ with new insights. As a result of Rahner's transcendental Christology, he has been able to determine the elements necessary for the symbol to function as this unifying factor and to determine the content mediated by the symbol as well as the appropriate response to the symbol. For this reason we cannot understand what he says about the Sacred Heart unless we measure it against the background of his Christology. Much of the criticism of Rahner's writings on the Sacred Heart Devotion, criticism which in many cases

---

[30] Cf. *supra*, p. 68.

simply took what he had to say and measured it against the context of the usual "manual Christology" of the schools, is based on the failure to understand the background from which it was written.

When seen against its own proper background, however, the picture changes. We simply have to look at the role which Christ's humanity plays in Rahner's Christology to get some idea of the difference. If the humanity of Jesus is the historical appearance of the Saviour, if the humanity of Jesus is the categorical reality of the Logos, if the humanity of Jesus is the absolute self-disclosure of God to man, if the humanity of Jesus represents the fulfillment of man's hope to find the sense of his existence, if the humanity of Jesus is instrumental in the eschatological fulfillment of that hope, then in the return to the experienced reality of a relationship to Christ it is entirely to be expected that his humanity should play a role in that lived faith experience. And if one part of Jesus' humanity, namely, his Heart, can serve as a natural primordial symbol to present all of these elements to us in a unified way by presenting us with the original unity of his person, and thereby elicit an appropriate response of love from us, then we have discovered both the justification and the central meaning of Devotion to the Sacred Heart.

3.2.0. RAHNER'S CHRISTOLOGY FROM BELOW: INTRODUCTION

As we noted previously, the discussion of the theology of the Devotion to the Sacred Heart takes place within the framework of an incarnational Christology from above. In recent years, however, there has been a noted shift in the Christological discussion, both in Catholic and Protestant circles. Some of the reasons for this shift may be found in such theological trends as the "God is Dead" theology of the 1960's, in "political theology" where there is a decided focus on Jesus as a social and political reformer (and sometimes on nothing more), and in a kind of fundamentalist religious revival which evidences itself in such "movements" as the so-called "Jesus people."

Each of these theological trends has as a common trait the return to the "Jesus of the Gospels" for its inspiration. Because of the problems and questions raised by such theological trends, it is only natural that Christology, as a theological discipline, should seek to address them. In doing so, Christology must first face the question of precisely what emerges from modern exegesis on the topic of what we know about the earthly life of Jesus. Secondly, Christology must face the question, or perhaps raise the question, of the historical grounding of faith in Jesus Christ, the traditional preserve of fundamental theology. Thirdly, in a specifically dogmatic way, Christology must ask the question of the relationship between the Church's magisterial tradition and the results of such an exegesis and fundamental theology. Fourthly, and as a result of this process, Christology must address the implied or express teaching about Jesus Christ which is contained in those new theological trends.

This brief sketch of the present situation makes it obvious that the starting point of Christology has changed. It is no longer sufficient to simply state that "the Word became flesh" and then to exegete that statement as the Church has done in the formulation of her Christological teaching. This is by no means a calling into question of the validity of that teaching. It is a statement of fact about the contemporary situation in which that teaching must take place. What is required is a dogmatic Christology capable of bridging the gap between exegetical-fundamental questions and the Church's tradition by developing concepts which are capable of doing justice to the demands of both, and which at the same time, are capable of addressing the issues raised about the meaning of Christ by the contemporary trends we mentioned above.

3.2.1.0. RAHNER'S CHRISTOLOGY FROM BELOW: PRESENTATION.

In developing a Christology from below, Rahner does not directly concern himself with the questions of exegesis and fundamental theology. He assumes certain data from these two fields, and by means of his transcendental Christology which we outlined above, he attempts to arrive at an understanding of the Church's tradition in terms of the concepts which he develops in that transcendental Christology. We shall present Rahner's attempt at a Christology from below under the following headings: starting point; exegetical data; fundamental data; transcendental deduction; categorical application; congruity with Tradition; relation to Theo-logy; communication of idioms; and soteriology.[31] In a second step we shall offer a brief critique

___

[31] These steps are implicit in the methodology which Rahner uses in this attempt. They are more or less explicitated at the end of his

of Rahner's attempt at a Christology from below, and finally we shall address the question of the (possible) relationship of such a Christology to the Devotion to the Heart of Crist.

3.2.1.1. *Starting Point: Faith Experience of Christ*

Rahner begins his Christology from below with a phenomenological approach. He simply states that our factually-lived relationship to Jesus Christ is a legitimate starting point for Christology, and then proceeds to clarify that relationship. Rahner means specifically that relationship as it is lived in the Christian Churches, i.e., a relationship of faith in Jesus Christ, as opposed to a "merely historical or human relationship." This relationship is to Jesus in his "original unity," that incorporates at one and the same time the elements of his inseity and his meaning for us. What specifies this faith relationship is the experience that in Jesus we encounter the mystery of God himself for the purpose of our redemption, so that Jesus himself is the Redeemer. The "givenness" of this factual relationship is what constitutes Christianity. Where *this* relationship ceases to exist, Christianity ceases. In the New Testament there is a plurality of Christologies, but *this* relationship of faith experience is common to and grounds each of them. The anthropological conditions for the possibility of this relationship must be expressed in a transcendental Christology. When this relationship to Christ is properly realized and understood, it so contains within itself its own *raison d'être* that it can neither be created nor built up from outside itself, for it is experienced precisely as a concrete absolute.[32]

3.2.1.2. *Exegetical Data*

This faith, as sketched above, must interest itself in the history of Jesus of Nazareth, since his historical person is the object of that faith. In approaching that history, we must be aware of the hermeneutic fact that what a person *is* and the extent to which he is able to verbalize what he is are two different poles. Thus in approaching the historical, pre-Easter Jesus we must say that his proclamation of himself cannot *contradict* what Christian faith believes about him. Nevertheless, we can-

treatise. Cf. Rahner and Thüsing, *Christologie — systematisch und exegetisch*, p. 59ff.

[32] *Ibid.*, p. 18f.

not *a priori* expect to find a complete convergence of Jesus'
pre-Easter understanding of himself and the content of the developed Christological faith of the Church. With this distinction
in mind, Rahner affirms the following as historical moments
in our knowledge of the pre-Easter Jesus:

1) Jesus lived in his religious milieu which he accepted as
divinely willed. His intention was to be a reformer of this milieu, not a religious revolutionary.

2) As a reformer, Jesus fought against an understanding of
the Law which put that Law in God's place, and against an ethic
of pious feeling and justification by works; his experience of
his nearness to God as Father led him to show solidarity with
the poor and outcast, but this was not intended as a direct critique of society in a sociological sense.

3) Jesus began his mission with hope of success, and in the
course of that mission grew in the awareness of the deadly
conflict he was engaged in with religious and political society.

4) Jesus faced his death with decisiveness and understood it
as a necessary consequence of fidelity to this mission.

5) Jesus wanted his disciples to follow him; in this discipleship the nearness of the Kingdom of God is also given to the
disciple; this discipleship, according to the mind of Jesus, does
not consist solely in explicit social committment.

6) *Historically*, the following questions may be considered
as open: whether Jesus used the title "Son of Man" of himself;
whether Jesus ascribed a soteriological meaning to his own
death; whether and in what sense he willed to establish a
Church.[33]

It is clear that as a result of this exegetical data, Rahner
is already assuming into a dogmatic Christology the ground for
rejecting or correcting the distortions of a strictly political theology which seeks to base itself on an alleged socio-political revolutionary mandate in the Gospels.

3.2.1.3. *Fundamental Questions: A "Consciousness" Christology*

According to Rahner, the task of a fundamental theology is
to be, essentially, a fundamental Christology. Thus this area of
theology must deal with the identity of the historical Jesus and
the Christ of faith who is proclaimed in the apostolic preaching
of the risen Lord. Secondly, a fundamental theology must pre-

---

[33] *Ibid.*, p. 25ff.

pare the anthropological ground for a transcendental Christology by identifying those areas in contemporary man's self-understanding which enable him to hear and accept the preaching of this Jesus as the risen Lord.

The key to establishing the identity of the historical Jesus and the risen Lord seems to lie in the development of a consciousness Christology. This means that an essential identity can be established between Jesus' understanding of himself as the one in whom the eschatological finality of the Kingdom of God — i.e., a new, final and decisive nearness of God to man as the critical situation in which man must decide for or against salvation — is present, and the Apostles' experience of Jesus as risen from the dead. In clarifying the resurrection experience of the Apostles, the following characteristics emerge:

1) Resurrection does not mean a simple return to life as it does in the miracles of the Old and New Testaments; it does mean the final "being saved" of the concrete historical human existence of Jesus by God; that concrete historical existence is neither his body nor his soul alone, but rather his whole person; it is not sufficient to interpret resurrection in terms of the "cause" of Jesus continuing after his death unless there is an essential connection between the continuance of his "cause" and the continuance of his person.

2) The apostolic witness to the resurrection of Jesus is not unified, but seeks to express itself in a variety of ways; in and through this variety it may be seen that the experience is not created by the Apostles, but comes from without; it is an experience which relates directly to Jesus as the Crucified One in his individuality and his fate in such a way that Jesus is experienced as saved and valid; this experience is available only in faith and grounds that faith itself; this experience of the resurrection is not to be continued in time, but is limited to a certain time span, so that witness is required to make that experience available to others.

The resurrection itself contributes to our knowledge of the person and work of Christ and is not simply the confirmation of something we knew about him before. This is obvious in the Gospel accounts of the pre-Easter Jesus. What emerges from the resurrection is the validation of the claim which the pre-Easter Jesus made for himself about the relationship between the Kingdom of God and his person. In this sense, Jesus is confirmed as the absolute Redeemer. New Testament Christologies are trying to express this experience in the various "mo-dels" they use, such as Prophet, Son and Logos. Thus they portray Jesus as the prophet who surpasses and dissolves the demands of the true prophet because he claims that his word is insurpassable; in him prophecy ends, not because God decides not to reveal himself any longer, but because in Jesus, God has so revealed himself that there is simply nothing more to be re-vealed. In this sense, too, Jesus is not *a* word of God, but *the* Word of God, *the* Logos. So, too, Jesus is not one in a long line of servants of God; he is *the* Son of God. Each of these predications has its origin in the identity between what Jesus proclaimed about himself (a proclamation which is based in his consciousness of himself) and what the resurrection experi-ence of the Apostles validates of Jesus himself.

From this consideration there emerges the fact of a unique relationship to God, and it is precisely that unique relationship between Jesus and God which lies behind the New Testament Christologies of Prophet, Son, and Logos. This same unique re-lationship also lies behind the classical expressions of Christol-ogy. The preservation of that unicity must be of prime im-portance in any attempt to develop a new Christological formula-tion. Any merely historical or human relationship to Jesus which is not based on his unique relationship to God is not sufficient. Thus a "Jesus people" approach to Christ which ignores this foundation of his unique relationship to God can not be con-sidered sufficient for the truly believing Christian.[34]

A fundamental theology must also concern itself with the anthropological condition for the possibility of hearing and ac-cepting this proclamation of the resurrection of Jesus in a faith relationship. Rahner locates that condition in every man's search for the assurance that he himself can achieve the lasting validity of his own self. What he is looking for is the assurance that the self which he experiences in his life history will somehow remain. This hope is not realized in the natural immortality of the soul, because man experiences himself as more than merely a spiritual soul. Nor does the composite body-soul existence in history satisfy this hope, since man is always confronted with his transcendence in this historical existence. Man must either affirm or deny the possibility of finding the fulfillment of this search. If he affirms it, he is faced with two choices: either

---

[34] *Ibid.*, pp. 28-38 and 42-47.

a continuing search for its historical realization, or the acknow-
ledgment of it having been experienced and discovered in faith.

This anthropological condition is that existential element
in man which enables him to accept the resurrection of Jesus.
Rahner says that fundamental theology may help man to reflect
upon the existence of this condition by reflecting on three experiences of contemporary man: the transcendent experience of
love of neighbor, the question of facing death, and the implicit
hope for the future whch is involved in planning.[35]

What is found in the apostolic preaching about the resurrection of Jesus is the categorical realization of man's transcendental hope for lasting validity. In this way, the faith which accepts Jesus as the absolute Saviour in whom man's hope for
validity is realized is an apostolic faith, rooted in the Apostles'
witness to what they experienced of Jesus in the resurrection.
Man can hear of it, because it corresponds to an exigency of his
human condition, and he can accept it as realized in Jesus because of the grace of God which is present in that apostolic
preaching itself.[36]

In a real sense, the foregoing considerations only form the
preamble to a truly *dogmatic* Christology from below. However,
the material which we considered under exegetical and fundamental data is precisely the data from which a Christology from
below must be developed. Our knowledge of the historical
Jesus, a knowledge which emerges primarily in his consciousness
of himself and his mission, is that area in which the concerns
of exegesis, fundamental theology and dogmatic theology all
converge. The proper concern of a dogmatic theology is to develop concepts in which this consciousness Christology can be
more universally expressed. A dogmatic Christology retains its
identity with this data because of the identity of consciousness
and being. In principle, each of the statements of a consciousness Christology are capable of translation into ontological categories, and vice versa. That "translation" takes place, according
to Rahner, in a transcendental Christology.[37]

---

[35] *Ibid.*, pp. 38ff. and 59-63. Cf. *idem*, "The Quest for Approaches Leading to an Understanding of the Mystery of the God-Man Jesus," *TI*, XIII,
p. 195ff.

[36] *Ibid.*, pp. 40ff.

[37] *Ibid.*, p. 63f. Cf. *idem*, "Remarks on the Importance of the History
of Jesus for Catholic Dogmatics," *TI* XIII, p. 201ff.

3.2.1.4. *Transcendental Deduction*

We have already presented the basic structure of Rahner's transcendental deduction of the concepts of absolute salvific event and absolute Saviour at the end of Section I of this chapter.[38] Rather than repeat that material, we will limit our discussion to the function of this transcendental deduction in the context of a Christology from below.

A transcendental Christology is basically a theological anthropology in a specifically Christological context. From a fundamental theology it takes the fact of man's desire for lasting validity and seeks the conditions of the possibility for its fulfillment. First it asks the foundation of this hope, and it sees its ontological basis in the *desiderium naturale visionis Dei,* man's natural desire to see God. Thus a theological anthropology understands man in terms of his radical orientation toward God, as obediential potentiality. The second condition for the possibility of the fulfillment of this potentiality is to be found in man's radically historical nature. Because he is a unique composite of spirit and matter, the fulfillment of this potentiality must be mediated to man materially, in time and space, and so historically.

Thus man must look for an historical event, most properly a human historical event, in which he can find this fulfillment. From this, a transcendental Christology deduces the characteristics of an absolute historical event in which God reveals himself for man's salvation through an absolute Saviour. These concepts clarify what it is that man is looking for. They do not of themselves point to its fulfillment. To achieve this, there must be a categorical return to the data of exegesis and fundamental theology.[39]

3.2.1.5. *Categorical Return to the Data*

In this categorical return to the data of exegesis and fundamental theology, the primary concern is to show that in Jesus of Nazareth we find the fulfillment of the requirements of absolute salvific event and absolute Saviour as they were deduced in the transcendental deduction. These requirements are fulfilled in him, and in him alone, because Jesus had a consciousness of

---

[38] Cf. *supra,* p. 108ff.
[39] Rahner and Thüsing, *Christologie — systematisch und exegetisch,* p. 20.

fulfilling this function during his lifetime and because that consciousness which he communicated to the disciples is revealed
as perfected and validated by God in the resurrection.[40]

3.2.1.6. *Relation to Tradition*

Since the Tradition which is incorporated in the Church's
magisterium is the test of the validity of any Christological statement, the results of this development of new concepts about
Christ must be confronted with the test of that Tradition. Therefore, the next step in developing a Christology from below must
be to show that these new concepts *de facto* express the same
thing which that Tradition expresses with its concepts.

The key to demonstrating this correspondence lies in properly thinking through the character of *absoluteness* which is predicated of both the event itself and the bearer of the event.
The events of human history are open-ended. What man does
in history can never achieve the character of absoluteness. Thus
if this event in history is to be truly absolute, it must be the
event of God himself. The categoriality of the event, i.e., the
Saviour, in his humanity must be the reality of God himself.
Only in this way can absoluteness be properly predicated of the
event and the Saviour. According to Rahner, in saying this we
have arrived at the point of identity between a Christology from
below and classical Christology. What classical Christology
sought to express by Hypostatic Union is expressed in a Christology from below in terms of absolute salvific event realized by
an absolute Saviour. Rahner implies that the new formulation
has an advantage over classical Christology inasmuch as it contains within itself a clearer understanding of the unity of the
person and the salvific function of Christ, hence a clearer understanding of the relationship between Christology and soteriology.[41] We will address the soteriology of this Christology from
below in the last section of our presentation of Rahner's thought.

3.2.1.7. *Relation to Theo-logy*

The question of the necessity of the pre-existence of God
in relation to this creaturely expression of himself in the world
is the opening to relate this new Christological formulation to
the doctrine of the Trinity. If this creaturely reality is God's

---

[40] *Ibid.*, p. 64.
[41] *Ibid.*, p. 66.

own reality in the world, this relationship of pre-existence is different from God's (general) pre-existence to all created reality. It is up to exegetes to determine more exactly the implications of the title Son when applied to Jesus. But if Jesus' consciousness of himself includes the consciousness of a special relationship to God, and if in the historicity of his humanity there is to be found the self-revelation of God as the subject of that humanity, then we can conclude to the identity of that subject with the "self-expressibility" of God as an immanent relationship in God himself. At this point the question actually becomes a question of trinitarian Theology, but it is one more indication, borne out through the history of the Tradition itself, of the mutual relationship between the development of concepts in both trinitarian and Christological reflection.[42]

3.2.1.8. *Communication of Idioms: the "Death of God"?*

A Christology from below must deal with the problems and heretical viewpoints raised by a "God is Dead" theology. The death of Jesus must interest us as a moment in the revelation through Incarnation itself and not simply in its salvific effects. Basically this involves a kind of contemporary communication of idioms applied to a very specific question. It would certainly be heretical to say that God died in the death of Jesus. Nevertheless, it is certainly incomplete to attribute the death of Jesus to his human nature and thereby imply that it has nothing to do with God himself. If it is true that God does not die in himself, nevertheless the death of Jesus must be seen in its relationship to the revelation of God himself in what he freely decided to be for us. This leads us to a theology of the death of Jesus, wherein the soteriological Tradition of the Church must seek to find its legitimate expression in terms of this new Christology from below.[43]

3.2.1.9. *Soteriology: the Salvific Meaning of the Death of Jesus as a Constitutive Moment of the Revelation Itself*

New Testament Christology attributes a saving meaning to the death of Jesus. His death is viewed precisely as the cause of our salvation, and this causality is understood in the categories of a sacrifice. In light of the difficulties raised about the mean-

---

[42] *Ibid.,* p. 68.
[43] *Ibid.,* p. 69.

ing of that sacrifice, Rahner asks whether or not it would be possible to develop a soteriology based on the death of Christ as it is viewed from the point of view of the resurrection. Since the sacrificial understanding of the New Testament is a theological construct which was developed to help men of those times to understand the salvific meaning of the death of Christ, it should be at least theoretically possible to arrive at a contemporary theological construct which would accomplish the same function for men of our times.

Rahner attempts to do this in terms of the connection between life-death-resurrection which we saw in Chapter II.[44] The meaning of life is expressed most fully in the act of dying. In his death Jesus most perfectly expresses that free and obedient relationship to God which he is in his very nature. The resurrection of Jesus is the revelation of the perfection of that life and death in and through which God is revealing himself.

Behind all of this stands God's purely gratuitous salvific will. That will creates for itself its human expression by positing the life of Jesus. That life in turn perfects itself in death. Thus the life and death of Jesus are the real causes of the salvific will of God, causes of what Rahner calls a quasi-sacramental, real-symbolical nature. In other words, the reality of God's salvific will posits its own other, its own real symbol, which is the life and death of Jesus. It realizes itself in the positing. That realization is what is revealed in the resurrection. Thus the soteriological significance of the Jesus-event itself can be seen in the act of his death if we understand that death in relation to his life and to the resurrection.[45]

3.2.2. CRITIQUE

This presentation of Rahner's Christology from below has been, at best, schematic. We have imposed our own structure on it in order to present its various aspects. Throughout this presentation Rahner keeps referring to open questions and to areas that need to be developed. In a sense we cannot criticize Rahner for the preliminary character of his presentation, for that is the goal he set for himself — namely, to work out a start of some kind for an orthodox Christology from below. Further-

---

[44] Cf. *supra*, p. 84ff.
[45] Rahner and Thüsing, *Christologie — systematisch und exegetisch*, p. 49.

more, the present state of the discussion would not allow for
much more than that, considering the newness of this Christological viewpoint.

The question which faces us here is this: is this really a
Christology from below? The question seems to be a fair one,
since in light of the presentation we made above we can see that
the key to Rahner's attempt is still a transcendental Christology.
Is this attempt at a new Christological viewpoint really successful? Certainly, in comparison to his older Christology, as we
presented it in Chapter II, the starting point of this Christology
from below is much less abstract, and consciously seeks to pay
more attention to the historical Jesus.

Nevertheless, in our opinion this attempt is not successful.
In order to arrive at a specifically dogmatic Christology from
below, Rahner has recourse to his own transcendental Christology. The deduction of the idea of an absolutely salvific event
and an absolute Saviour makes sense in terms of his own
theological viewpoint. However, it is legitimate to ask if this
is what is meant by a Christology from below. The weakness
in Rahner's system is precisely the question of the categorical
return to the history of Jesus of Nazareth. Does this history
have meaning in itself, or does it have meaning only in terms
of the transcendental categories which can be developed out of
it? It would seem that the primary concern of a Christology
from below must be to show that the categorical, the historical
aspect of Jesus of Nazareth *in itself*, as it emerges from the New
Testament, engenders faith and is supported by the findings of
exegesis, contains within itself all the elements of an orthodox
Christology. Rahner's proposal, in the very fact that it relies
on the transcendental deduction to arrive at the point of an
orthodox Christology, seems to call that sufficiency into question.

One of the basic elements of all of Rahner's thought is the
dialectical relationship between the transcendental and the categorical-historical. To understand what Rahner is saying, one
must be aware that the categorical, as it is present in the existential situation which is the starting point of much of Rahner's
theology, is in most cases simply presumed. As a result of his
transcendental deductions, Rahner is often able to return to the
categorical with new insights and a more precise understanding.
We saw this method operate both in his writings on the Devotion to the Sacred Heart and in his older Christology.

This dialectic is still operative in his attempt at a Christology from below. However, Rahner seems to ignore a very im-

portant piece of data in his reconstruction of the categoriality of Jesus of Nazareth. What he says about the exegetical data and our knowledge of the historical Jesus is correct as far as it goes. But it leaves out of the picture the very specific relationship of Jesus with God as his Father.[46] As a result, when we arrive at the point of the question of pre-existence, it is not clear that the subject we are speaking of is precisely the Logos, and not simply God. True, Rahner, identifies this subject with the "self-expressibility" of God in an immanent, trinitarian relationship. But when he considers the categoriality of Jesus, he leaves the expression of that relationship in the life of Jesus out of the picture.[47]

On the positive side we must point out that one of Rahner's chief concerns in approaching the question of a Christology from below is to show that a simple Jesuology is not sufficient to meet the demands of Catholic orthodoxy.[48] From many of the remarks he made concerning contemporary faith experience and fundamental theology we can judge that demonstration to be successful.

Also of a positive nature are the anthropological considerations which Rahner adds to the fundamental theological basis of a Christology from below. His analysis of three experiences, namely, love of neighbor, the question of one's own death, and man's hope for the future, which are factors in man's experience of his search for lasting validity, an experience which can lead contemporary man to search for and find Jesus Christ as Saviour, are certainly a positive contribution to the discussion.

In general we would say that Rahner's attempt is valuable, even if it does not succeed, because he analyzes properly those factors which must go into the development of a Christology from below. He correctly points out the positions which must be avoided because they are insufficient; he is on the right track with regards to the scriptural and fundamental data which must be a part of a Christology from below; and he correctly posits the role of the Church's Tradition, especially as that Tradition is formulated in the Chalcedonian teaching, as the ultimate test of the validity of the results of any new Christological formulation.

---

[46] This reflects Thüsing's criticism of Rahner's exegetical data. *Ibid.*, pp. 133ff.

[47] B. van den Heijden, *op. cit.*, pp. 406ff.

[48] Interview with Karl Rahner, December 21, 1975.

3.2.3.0. *The Relationship of a Christology from Below to the Theology of the Devotion to the Sacred Heart*

In this section we propose to ask the question of whether, and if so, how, this Christology from below is related, or capable of being related, to the theology of the Devotion to the Sacred Heart. We ask this question because we believe, with Rahner, that if the Christological discussion of Catholic theologians has shifted to this Christological viewpoint, then any attempts to write about the theology of the Devotion to the Sacred Heart must reflect this shift.[49]

3.2.3.1. *The Problem*

The problem, as we see it, is whether the symbolization of Christ as it is proposed under the symbol of the Sacred Heart, is still viable in this changed Christological situation. Let us specify this problem.

1) First, we must determine to what extent this Christology reflects an already accomplished shift in the lived faith experience of the Church.

2) Second, we must determine to what extent such a shift in the faith experience of Jesus, if this shift *de facto* exists, plays or has played a role in the discomfiture of many Catholics with Devotion to the Sacred Heart.

3) Third, we must determine which elements, if any, of a Christology from below are compatible with the symbol of the Heart of Christ.

4) Fourth, if we find compatible elements, we must seek to integrate them into the actual practice of the Devotion.

We do not pretend to be in a position to answer each of these aspects of the problem. However, we hope to make a few remarks about each of these aspects which will contribute to the discussion.

3.2.3.2. *The Faith Experience of Jesus Christ*

To what extent does a Christology from below reflect a change in the faith experience of Jesus? From a formal point of view we would suggest that it does not reflect a change in faith experience. By faith experience we mean that living relationship to Christ in the original unity of his inseity and his

---

[49] *Ibid.*

meaning for us which Rahner described in his phenomenological approach to that experience. It is this experience which is prior to all Christological reflection. This experience is of such a nature that it cannot be assumed completely and adequately into the concepts of theology. This is the basis for the distinction between faith and theology.

What has changed is the theological situation, and this change is conditioned by a changed pastoral situation. The formulations of the Council of Chalcedon are no longer pastorally viable. Hence theology has been compelled to search for new formulations which meet the double test of accessibility to contemporary man and adequacy of orthodox expression in terms of the Tradition.

Those who have this faith experience of Jesus in all probability have already searched for and found some unthematic conceptual expression of that faith experience. It is the task of a Christology from below to develop a formal, thematic conceptual expression of that experience.

We would suggest that the symbol of the Heart of Jesus, as Rahner has specifically determined that symbol, is and remains a valid expression in symbolic form of that faith experience. It is a valid expression precisely because it presents the Christian with Jesus Christ in the original unity of his inseity and his meaning for us. Hence what the Christian experiences in the symbol of the Heart of Christ is precisely that experience which Rahner posits as the legitimate starting point of a Christology from below. From this we conclude that an adequate Christology from below, in principle, should so help to clarify that experience that at the same time it would clarify what the Christian experiences in the Heart of Jesus.

3.2.3.3. *Disaffection with the Devotion*

If the symbol remains valid in expressing the faith experience, then we must look elsewhere to explain disaffection with the Devotion. Rahner and many others have pointed to the sentimentality of the depictions of the symbol, the effusive nature of some prayers to the Sacred Heart, and other causes of this discomfiture.[50] The disaffection seems to lie in the area of con-

---

[50] Cf. R. Gutzwiller, "The Opposition," in Stierli, *op. cit.*, p. 1ff., and J. Galot, "Quel est l'objet de la devotion au Sacré-Coeur?", *NRT* 77 (1955), 924.

veying the meaning of the experience of the symbol of the Heart
of Jesus into concrete forms of expression.

It would be important to determine if this disaffection is not
itself a reflection of the fact that Christians have found an unthematic expression of their faith experience of Christ and whether or not it is this unthematic expression which really lies
at the root of the experience of disaffection with the concrete
forms of the Devotion as they have been traditionally practiced
in the Church. Such a determination would help to clarify the
core of the problem which people seem to have with the Devotion today, and would be a major contribution in helping to
determine the nature of a solution to the problem.

3.2.3.4. *Compatibility of Elements*

Even if we judge Rahner's attempt at a Christology from
below to be unsuccessful, nevertheless he has clarified some essential elements which would compose such a Christology. In this
section we would like to propose three of those elements as
having a direct relationship to the symbol of the Heart of Christ.
Besides the validity of the symbol as an expression of the faith
experience of Christ, we would propose that the three considerations from a fundamental theology, namely, love of neighbor,
the question of one's own death, and man's hope for the future
are three elements of a Christology from below which could
easily be assumed into a theology of the Devotion to the Sacred
Heart. We will briefly show the compatibility between these
elements and the symbol of the Heart of Christ.[51]

1. *Love of Neighbor*: By love of neighbor Rahner means
that love which Jesus speaks of in Mt 25, a love which is identical with true love of God. Every act of love of another person
is an act of risk. Man risks giving himself entirely to another
in the hope that this risk is meaningful and will not be disappointed. This hope is ultimately fulfilled in the person of Jesus
himself. In Jesus the absolute love of man for God and the
absolute, salvific love of God for mankind are made visible. In
Christ this unity of the love of God and neighbor becomes a
reality. Because of the absolute character of his love, man can
come to know that his hope for the acceptance of his own acts
of love for another ultimately will not be disappointed, because

---

[51] Rahner and Thüsing, *Christologie — systematisch und exegetisch*,
p. 61ff.

God himself, in and through Christ, has accepted those acts of love as love of himself.

Because this unity is found in and "guaranteed" by the person of Christ, the symbol of his Heart can make that love present to us in its unity. In the Heart of Christ we find symbolized the absolute epitome of what it means to love God and man at one and the same time, in one act of love. In the Heart of Christ man can find symbolized the fulfillment of all the hope he has for his own acts of love. Because Jesus is at one and the same time the ground and the fulfillment of this kind of love, the symbol of his Heart, by making him present to us, presents us with him in the unity of this love.[52]

2. *The Question of Death*: How do we face the question of our own death? Do we see it as the absolute absurd ending of our existence, and hence fight against it? Rahner says that a theology of death, derived from the categoriality of the death of Jesus, can enable us to face this question and find an answer which goes beyond the mere rejection of death. Death is the unique act of the end of life. It is unique because man, who experiences himself as the freedom to act, is suddenly faced with a situation in which he must passively face the inevitability of the end of his existence in this world. How can we make sense out of this dialectic? Rahner proposes that a theology of the death of Jesus provides the answer. Jesus accepted this ambiguity as a reality in his own life. And because he is at the same time divine, and therefore the ultimate ground of this ambiguity itself, in accepting it as his own reality he gives meaning to it.[53]

The fact, therefore, that Jesus faced death in all the ambiguity of the act of dying gives meaning to our facing of our own death with the courageous and obedient acceptance, as our own free act, of the passivity involved in the act of dying. This relationship between the death of Jesus and our own death can find its symbolization in the Heart of Christ. The fact that the prime biblical foundation of the symbol is the piercing of the side of the dead Christ would seem to justify saying that the death of Christ is an intimate part of the symbol itself. In fact, it is by the act of his death that Jesus reveals himself in

---

[52] *Ibid.*, p. 61, and *idem*, "The Quest for Approaches ...," *TI* XIII, p. 211f.

[53] *Ibid.*, p. 62, and *idem*, "The Quest for Approaches ...," *TI* XIII, p. 212f.

the fulness of his meaning for us. If in fact we Christians are called upon to die with Christ, to die into his death in order to rise into his resurrection, then the Christian meaning of the individual death of each Christian can find itself incorporated into the symbol of the Heart of Christ.

To this consideration of the death of Christ in the context of a fundamental theology we could join a consideration of what Rahner says about the death of Christ as the real symbol of the salvific will of God. The death of Christ is that real symbolic "other" which makes present to us the salvific will of God as the ultimate ground of our salvation. If the death of Christ is a constitutive element of the symbol of the Heart itself, then this salvific meaning of the death of Christ, as the proper soteriological element of a Christology from below, would also be conveyed by the symbol of the Heart.[54]

3. *The Hope for the Future*: One of the experiences of modern man is his hope for the future, a hope that expresses itself in such structures as planning. Implied in this planning is the hope that man's history will continue to be a development of man himself and of his domination of the world. Rahner interprets this fact as a sign of man's hope that by creating better conditions, he may be better able to overcome the discrepancy which he experiences within himself between what he is and what he could and should be. Man seeks the fulfillment of this hope within his history, and according to Rahner, it is only the revelation of Jesus that prevents that search from becoming an ideology. In Christ, God has revealed *himself* to be the absolute future of man.[55]

Inasmuch as the symbol of the Heart of Jesus is the heart of the glorified Lord, we can say that the symbol can represent to man, in terms of this hope for the future, the fulfillment of what he hopes to become. Thus in seeing the symbol of the Heart of Jesus, man can come to realize that all of his striving in history has as its goal the divinization of man in the beatific vision.

---

[54] Cf. *supra*, p. 122f.
[55] Rahner and Thüsing, *Christologie — systematisch und exegetisch*, p. 62f., and *idem*, "The Quest for Approaches ...," *TI* XIII, p. 214.

3.2.3.5. *Integration into the Devotion*

If the relationship between elements of a Christology from below and the symbol of the Sacred Heart which we sketched in the previous section is a valid one, then these elements can and should be integrated into the Devotion itself. Just how that can be achieved remains a question. But if these are valid insights about Christology, the symbol and contemporary man, they should certainly find a reflection in the practice of the Devotion. Perhaps they could serve as principles for meditation and could find expression in terms of new, updated prayers to the Sacred Heart. One thing is certain: if the Devotion to the Heart of Christ is to regain its popularity within the Church, it must begin to reflect the kind of thinking which is involved in a Christology from below.

3.2.4.0. A REFLECTION ON THE DIFFERENT FUNCTIONS OF THE SYMBOL

As we saw in the first section of Chapter III, the Heart of Christ has an important symbolic function in terms of a metaphysical or transcendental Christology. In the context of Christology whose major emphasis is the divinity of Christ, the Heart of Christ serves to make the totality of Christ present in the unity of his divine-human reality and his salvific meaning for us. It has the powerful function as a symbol to present the unity of Christ to us both as an anterior expression of the lived faith experience and as a posterior corrective to any one-sidedness that may result from the perspective of traditional Christology from above.

We would propoes that it retains this symbolic function in the context of a Christology from below. As we saw above, it is a valid symbolization of the faith experience which is the starting point of a Christology from below. If that Christology concentrates on the humanity of Christ in his categorical-historical aspects, there is certainly the possibility of a one-sidedness on the other extreme, namely, a concentration on the humanity of Christ in such a way that the divinity becomes unclear. In this context the Heart of Christ could preserve its symbolic function by presenting us with the unity of Christ in such a way that the human elements are seen preicsely as the expression of the divinity, and thus again function as a corrective against this possibility.

3.2.5.0. SUMMARY

In this chapter we have shown the relationship of the symbol of the Heart of Christ, as Rahner has determined it, to the individual elements of two different Christological contexts as he has developed them. Even if we judge the second context of a Christology from below to be unsuccessful, we have pointed out what we consider valid considerations which Rahner has made for a Christology from below. It is these elements which we related to the symbol of the Heart of Christ.

Throughout this work we have limited ourselves to a consideration of the thought of Karl Rahner. We believe that what we have arrived at is a picture of the harmony between his Christology and his writings on the Sacred Heart. Not all the elements are capable of complete harmonization. Nevertheless, on the whole this harmony does exist.

If we were to choose another theologian's work, the picture of this relationship would probably be quite different. In terms of this specific relationship between the Christology and the theology of Devotion to the Sacred Heart of Karl Rahner, we would like to conclude this thesis by offering some brief reflections on the relationship between theology and spirituality as they emerge from the relationship which we have illustrated throughout this work.

CONCLUSION: SOME REFLECTIONS ON THE RELATIONSHIP BETWEEN THEOLOGY AND SPIRITUALITY AS THEY HAVE EMERGED FROM THIS STUDY

4.0. INTRODUCTION

The proces of this thesis has been two-fold. In the first two chapters we limited ourselves to an exposition of the theology of Devotion to the Sacred Heart and the Christology of Karl Rahner. The third chapter was synthetic, pointing out the relationships that exist between these two areas of Rahner's thought. Implicit in this synthesis are some relationships between theology and spirituality. As a conclusion to this work we would like to make some of those relationships explicit and make a few comments about them.

4.1.0. THE PRIORITY OF RELIGIOUS EXPERIENCE

Christian religious experience, the faith relationship to Jesus Christ, is the proper starting point for both dogmatic and spiritual theology. That faith experience itself is intuitive and unthematic. It is the task of both dogmatic and spiritual theology to develop concepts and structures which aid man in understanding the content and nature of that faith experience.

We have seen this priority of faith experience operative in the starting point of Rahner's writings. The starting point for his reflection on the Devotion to the Heart of Christ was the existential experience of the Devotion. This led to the development of his theology of symbolism as a necessary clarification of one aspect of that experience. The difficulties experienced by many people in practicing the Devotion led to a theological reflection on the elements of the Devotion, from which a reinterpretation of the practices of the Devotion became possible.

The starting point of his Christology, whether from above or from below, is the actual situation of believing Christians.

In the case of a Christology from above, this led to the recognition of the basic problems involved in classical Christology, namely, the possibility inherent in that Christology of a monophysite bias. If there is any one theme which runs through Rahner's Christology it is a concern that concepts be developed which will enable Christians to understand their faith in Christ in an existentially and intellectually orthodox manner. In the case of a Christology from below, it was an analysis of the current situation, with its heretical and defective conceptualizations of Christ, which led to the attempt to develop a Christology from below with concepts that would be both orthodox and understandable to contemporary man.

In all of this, Rahner has insisted on the priority of religious experience. This priority is operative in the existential considerations which form his starting point; it is operative in the *a priori* hermeneutical realization that no concept or structure can ever completely and adequately express the complexity of the experience itself; it is operative in allowing the experience of Christ in faith to be a real criteriological principle for judging the adequacy or inadequacy of the results of theological reflection.

Theology and spirituality relate to this faith experience in different ways. The task of theology is to analyze the content of this faith experience in terms of the Tradition and magisterium of the Church. Spirituality is more directly concerned with the experience itself. It seeks to reflect upon that experience in such a way as to explain the experience in terms of its constitutive elements. Because both are related to the one faith experience, they are related to each other. We will seek to explain that relationship in our third conclusion. Both endeavors, however, are subject to the original faith experience as starting point, hermeneutical principle, and as standard of judgment.

4.2.0. SYMBOL AS THE PROPER EXPRESSION OF RELIGIOUS EXPERIENCE

Because this faith experience by its very nature eludes complete and adequate conceptualization, it finds its proper expression in the symbol. By symbol we mean precisely that notion of symbolism which Rahner has developed, the notion of the real symbol. Despite the rationalistic tendencies of human thought, symbols must be seen as a necessary and meaningful part of man's attempt to understand his experience, including especially his religious experience. The symbol, and only the symbol, provides man with the means to deal with this faith experience in a *humanly* meaningful way. Man experiences himself as an existential unity. Only the symbol provides man with the means of expressing the unity of his religious experience in terms of his own existential unity.

From this point of view we can conclude with Rahner that both dogmatic and spiritual theology can become more effective in their attempts at conceptualizing this faith experience only if they learn to appreciate in an existential way the real communicative nature of real symbols. While both theology and spirituality must reflect on the content of these symbols, they must also recognize the secondary, derivative nature of the concepts they employ to express the content of those symbols. We could express the difference between symbols and concepts in the following terms: real symbols communicate to man in the original unity of his own being the original unity of his religious experience; as such, symbols reach man in the unity of his intellectual, volitional and affective relationship to all of reality; concepts, on the other hand, are fundamentally intellectual abstractions; as such they are necessary for man to understand the content of what the symbol presents him with; they lack the same power which a symbol has to involve man in the unity of his volitional and affective aspects.

4.3.0. THE MUTUAL RELATIONSHIP BETWEEN THEOLOGY AND SPIRITUALITY

Because both dogmatic theology and spirituality share a common starting point in the faith experience, and because both dogmatic theology and spirituality share a derivation from the common symbols which express that religious experience, there is a mutual determining effect between these two branches of theology. In fact, this has been a presupposition of this entire work, and we believe that it is borne out in the results.

If we look at the presentation made in this thesis, we can see this relationship illustrated. A theological reflection on the Devotion to the Sacred Heart necessarily is dependent upon a Christology to develop those concepts by which it can judge itself in terms of the completeness and adequacy of what this specifically *devotional* expression of the faith experience is bearing witness to. At the same time, a Christology is dependent

upon that devotional expression of faith, such as we find in the
Devotion to the Sacred Heart, in order to arrive back at the
original unity of the faith experience of Jesus Christ which it
attempts to conceptualize. Neither can exist independently of
the other.

Furthermore, if the faith experience is a legitimate starting
point for theology, then the reflection on that faith experience
which is the proper realm of spirituality must be a constitutive
part of those elements on which a theological reflection is based.
In other words, if spirituality reflects upon the faith experience
and determines it to be of such and such a nature, this result
of the reflection of spiritual theology must be incorporated into
the data on which a dogmatic theology bases its own proper
reflection.

At the same time, in the categorical return which is necessary
to complete any theological reflection, the clarification which is
wrought by the conceptualization of dogmatic theology must be
incorporated into the work of spiritual theology. This clarification may serve either an enlightening and deepening function,
or a corrective function.

4.4.0. SPIRITUALITY AND CHRISTIAN ANTHROPOLOGY

One of the essential elements of Rahner's theology is his
theological anthropology. This anthropology in turn is conditioned by the Christological insights which he has developed.
A properly Christian understanding of man can only be achieved
by a proper understanding of the reality of the human nature of
Christ as the transcendental and categorical pinnacle of the
realization of human existence. It is this viewpoint which enables
Rahner, in terms of his own theological system, to avoid the
monophysite bias of classical Christology.

The fulness of this anthropological viewpoint must be applied to spirituality. As the history of spirituality amply de-
monstrates, there is always the danger within spirituality of so
concentrating on the spirit-element in man that it forgets or
overlooks the fact that man is a unique reality of matter and
spirit. If spirituality necessarily concentrates on man's faith
experience, in which he experiences his transcendence in a most
radical way, it must always seek to be conscious of the fact
that this transcendent experience is necessarily mediated in and
through the categoriality of man's concrete, historical existence.

The concrete, historical humanity of Jesus must always be before the eyes of the spiritual theologian. It is in and through the humanity of Jesus that we come to know God as he is and wishes to be for us. It is in and through the humanity of Christ that we have communion with the Father through the Spirit. The humanity of Christ is the eternal model and fulfillment of what Christian man is and must be because of God's grace. If the goal of the spiritual life, of life in the Spirit, is to become so like Christ that we enjoy union with God through his grace, then the humanity of Christ must always stand before us as a sign and a challenge of what we are and what we must become.

SELECT BIBLIOGRAPHY

1. *Works of Karl Rahner*

RAHNER, Karl, *Biblical Homilies*. New York, 1966.
——, *The Dynamic Element in the Church*. Translated by W. J. O'Hara. New York, 1964.
——, *Encounters with Silence*. Translated by J. Demske. Westminster, Md., 1960.
——, *The Eternal Year*. Translated by J. Shea. London, 1964.
——, *Everyday Faith*. Translated by W. J. O'Hara. London, 1968.
——, *Free Speech in the Church*. No translator given. New York, 1960.
——, *Geist in Welt*. 2nd Edition. Edited by J. B. Metz. Munich, 1957. English translation: *Spirit in the World*. Translated by W. Dych. New York, 1968.
——, *Grace in Freedom*. Translated and adapted by H. Graef. New York, 1969.
——, *Hörer des Wortes*. 2nd Edition. Edited by J. B. Metz. Munich, 1963. English translation: *Hearers of the Word*. Translated by M. Richards. New York, 1969.
——, *Hominisation*. Vol. XIII of *Quaestiones Disputatae*. Translated by W. T. O'Hara. New York, 1965.
——, *Mission and Grace*. Translated by C. Hastings. London, 1966.
——, *Nature and Grace and Other Essays*. Translated by D. Wharton. London, 1963.
——, *On Prayer*. No translator given. New York, 1958.
——, *The Priesthood*. Translated by E. Quinn. New York, 1973.
——, *Schriften zur Theologie*. Vol. I. Freiburg, 1954. English translation: *Theological Investigations*. Vol. I. Translated by C. Ernst. London, 1961.
——, *Schriften zur Theologie*. Vol. II. Freiburg, 1955. English Translation: *Theological Investigations*. Vol. II. Translated by K.-H. Kruger. London, 1963.
——, *Schriften zur Theologie*. Vol. III. Freiburg, 1956. English Translation: *Theological Investigations*. Vol. III. Translated by K.-H. and B. Kruger. London, 1963.
——, *Schriften zur Theologie*. Vol. IV. Freiburg, 1962. English Translation: *Theological Investigations*. Vol. IV. Translated by K. Smyth. London, 1966.
——, *Schriften zur Theologie*. Vol. V. Freiburg, 1964. English Translation: *Theological Investigations*. Vol. V. Translated by K.-H. Kruger. London, 1966.
——, *Schriften zur Theologie*. Vol. VI. Freiburg, 1965. English Translation: *Theological Investigations*. Vol. VI. Translated by K.-H. and B. Kruger. London, 1969.

————, *Schriften zur Theologie*. Vol. VII. Freiburg, 1966. English Translation: *Theological Investigations*. Vol. VII. Translated by D. Bourke. London, 1971. Pages 11 through 282 of the German Edition. Vol. VIII. Translated by D. Bourke. London, 1971. Pages 283 through 515 of the German Edition.

————, *Schriften zur Theologie*. Vol. VIII. Freiburg, 1967. English Translation: *Theological Investigations*. Vol. IX. Translated by G. Harrison. London, 1972. Pages 13 through 326 of the German Edition. Vol. X. Translated by D. Bourke. London, 1973. Pages 327 through 707 of the German Edition.

————, *Schriften zur Theologie*. Vol. IX. Freiburg, 1970. English Translation: *Theological Investigations*. Vol. XI. Translated by D. Bourke. London, 1974. Pages 11 through 335 of the German Edition. Vol. XII. Translated by D. Bourke. London, 1974. Pages 339 through 590 of the German Edition.

————, *Schriften zur Theologie*. Vol. X. Freiburg, 1972. English Translation: *Theological Investigations*. Vol. XIII. Translated by D. Bourke. London, 1975. Pages 11 through 238 of the German Edition.

————, *Schriften zur Theologie*. Vol. XI. Freiburg, 1973.

————, *Schriften zur Theologie*. Vol. XII. Freiburg, 1975.

————, *Servants of the Lord*. Translated by R. Strachan. New York, 1968.

————, *Spiritual Exercises*. Translated by K. Baker. New York, 1965.

————, *On the Theology of Death*. Vol. II of *Quaestiones Disputatae*. 2nd Edition. Translated by C. Henkey. New York, 1965.

————, *The Trinity*. Translation of *Mysterium Salutis*, Vol. II, Chapter 5. Translated by J. Donceel. New York, 1970.

————, *Visions and Prophecies*. Vol. X of *Quaestiones Disputatae*. Translated by C. Henkey and R. Strachan. New York, 1964.

————, *Watch and Pray with Me*. Translated by W. Dych. New York, 1966.

RAHNER, Karl, et al. *The Bible in a New Age*. London, 1965.

RAHNER, Karl, et al., eds. *Handbuch der Pastoraltheologie*. 4 vols. Freiburg, 1964-1969.

RAHNER, Karl, and RAHNER, Hugo. *Prayers for Meditation*. New York, 1962.

RAHNER, Karl, and RATZINGER, J. *Revelation and Tradition*. Vol. XVII of *Quaestiones Disputatae*. Translated by W. J. O'Hara. New York, 1966.

RAHNER, Karl, and THÜSING, W. *Christologie — systematisch und exegetisch*. Vol. LV of *Quaestiones Disputatae*. Freiburg, 1972.

RAHNER, Karl, and VORGRIMMLER, H. *Kleines theologisches Wörterbuch*. Freiburg, 1961. English Edition: *Concise Theological Dictionary*. Edited by C. Ernst. Translated by R. Strachan. New York, 1965.

RAHNER, Karl, "Begriffsbestimmung der Herz-Jesu Andacht im Lichte der theologischen Synthese." *Sesiones de Estudio del Primer Congreso internacional sobre el culto al sagrado corazón de Jesús*. Barcelona, 1964, 49-57.

————, "Coeur de Jesus chez Origène?" *Revue d'Ascetique et Mystique*, XIV (1934), 171-174.

————, "Geheimnis des Herzens." *Geist und Leben*, XX (1957), 161-165.

————, "Herz." *Handbuch theologischer Grundbegriffe*. Vol. I. 690-697.

———, "Jesus Christus II: Systematik der kirchlichen Christologie." *Lexikon für Theologie und Kirche*. 2nd Edition, 1958. Vol. V, Col. 953-961.

———, "Jesus Christ IV: History of Dogma and Theology." *Sacramentum Mundi*. Vol. III. 192-209.

———, "Priester und Herz-Jesu Verehrung." *Der Sendbote des Herzens Jesu*. XCIV (1967), 4-6; 27-28.

———, "Salvation," *Sacramentum Mundi*. Vol. V. 405-409; 416-432; 435-438.

2. Works on the Sacred Heart

Aa. Vv. *Le Coeur*. *Etudes Carmélitaines*. Toulouse, 1950.

BEA, A., et al., eds. *Cor Jesu*. 2 Vols. Rome, 1959.

DHORME, P. *L'Emploi métaphorique des noms de parties du corps en hébreu et en akkadien*. Paris, 1923.

DEGLI ESPOSTI, F. *La teologia del Sacro Cuore di Gesù*. Da Leone XIII a Pio XII. Rome, 1967.

HAMON, A. *Histoire de la Dévotion au Sacré-Coeur*. 5 Vols. Paris, 1923-1940.

LEDIT, J. *La Plaie du Côté*. Rome: Pont. Inst. Orientalium Studiorum, 1970.

NOUWENS, J., ed. *L'actualité d'un culte*. Rapports du Congres sur le Sacré-Coeur, Tilburg 3-5 juin, 1955. Tilburg, 1957.

PIUS XI, Pope. *Miserentissimus Redemptor*. Encyclical Letter of May 8, 1928. *Acta Apostolicae Sedis*. XX (1928), 165-178.

PIUS XII, Pope. *Haurietis Aquas*. Encyclical Letter of May 15, 1956. *Acta Apostolicae Sedis* XLVIII (1956), 309-353.

STIERLI, J., ed. *Cor Salvatoris*. Freiburg, 1954. English Translation: *Heart of the Saviour*. Translated by P. Andrews. New York, 1957.
Reviews:
H. Rondet. *Christus*. IV (Oct., 1954), 139.
M. G.(alli). *Orientierung*. XIX (1955), 131.
A. Ostiguy. *Sciences ecclésiastiques*. VII (1955), 229.
I.-A. Robillard. *La Vie Spirituelle*. XCV (1956), 209.
Reviews of K. Rahner's Article as Reprinted in *Schriften* III:
C.-J. Geffre. *Revue des Sciences philosophiques et théologiques*. XLI (1957), 544.
M. J. Donnelly. *Theological Studies*. XVIII (1957), 288.

RICHSTAETTER, K. *Das Herz des Welterlösers*. Freiburg, 1932.

TESSAROLO, A. *Il culto del Sacro Cuore a commento dell'enciclica "Haurietis Aquas."* Torino-Bologna, 1957.

VERHEYLEZOON, L. *Devotion to the Sacred Heart*. Westminster, Md., 1955.

BAUMGAERTEL, F., and BEHM, J. "Kardia." *TDNT*. Vol. III. Edited by G. Kittel. Grand Rapids, 1965. 605-613.

BORKOWSKI, S. von Dunin. "Leiden mit Christus." *Stimmen der Zeit*. CXVI (1929), 390.

CABASUT, A. "Coeurs (Changement des, Echange des)." *Dictionnaire de Spiritualité*. Vol. II. Cols. 1046-1051.

CALVERAS, J. "El simbolismo en el Corazón de Jesús, como objeto de culto." *Manresa*. XXII (1950), 34.

CLIFFORD, J. "The Proper Object of Devotion to the Sacred Heart." *Irish Ecclesiastical Record*. L (1937), 500-512.

GALOT, J. "Quel est l'objet de la dévotion au Sacré-Coeur." *Nouvelle Revue Théologique.* LXXVII (1955), 924-928.

GELPI, D. "Rahner's Theology of the Sacred Heart Devotion." *Woodstock Letters.* 1966. 405-417.

GRILLMEYER, A., "Theologia Cordis: Das Herz in Glaube und Frömmigkeit." *Geist und Leben.* XXI (1948), 332-351.

HAMON, A. "Coeur (Sacré)." *Dictionnaire de Spiritualité.* Vol. II. Cols. 1023-1046.

HEUFELDER, E. M., "Das Zeichen des Herzens." *Benediktiner Monatschrift.* XXXI (1955), 177-182.

MORGENROTH, A., "Devotion to the Sacred Heart and Modern Man." *Review for Religious.* XXIV (1965), 418-428.

MOTHERWAY, T. "The Proper Object of Devotion to the Sacred Heart." *Irish Ecclesiastical Record.* LI (1938), 147-158.

SOLANO, J. "La expresión 'Corazón de Jesús' en los documentos pontificios." *Manresa.* XXVII (1955), 291-310.

TUCCI, R. "Letteratura recente sulla devozione al S. Cuore di Gesù." *Civiltà Cattolica* (1957, Vol. I), 182-194.

ZORÉ, J. N. "Recentiorum quaestionum de cultu Ss. Cordis Jesu conspectus (utrum crisis an evolutio praevideatur)." *Gregorianum.* XXVII (1956), 104-120.

3. *Critical Works on Rahner's Theology*

BALTHASAR, H. U. v., *Cordula oder der Ernstfall.* Einsiedeln, 1966.

GELPI, D. *Light and Life.* New York, 1966.

LENIHAN, D. *The Transcendental Method of Karl Rahner as Applied to the Problem of God.* Exercitatio ad Licentiam. Rome: Pontifical Gregorian University, 1970 (unpublished).

McCOOL, G. *A Rahner Reader.* New York, 1975.

METZ, J. B., ed. *Gott in Welt.* Festgabe für Karl Rahner zum 60. Geburtstag. 2 Vols. Freiburg, 1964.

OCHS, R. *The Death in Every Now.* New York, 1969.

ROBERTS, L. *The Achievement of Karl Rahner.* New York, 1967.

SHEPHERD, W. *Man's Condition.* New York, 1969.

SPECK, J. *Karl Rahners theologische Anthropologie.* Munich, 1967.

VAN DER HEIJDEN, B. *Karl Rahner, Darstellung und Kritik seiner Grundposition.* Einsiedeln, 1973.

VORGRIMMLER, H., *Karl Rahner: His Life, Thought and Works.* Translated by E. Quinn. London, 1966.

AUER, J. "Das Werk Karl Rahners." *Theologische Revue.* LX (1964), 145-156.

BAKER, K. "Rahner: The Transcendental Method." *Continuum.* II (1964), 52-59.

BALTHASAR, H. U. v., "Grösse und Last der Theologie heute: einige grundsätzliche Gedanken zu zwei Aufsatzbänden Karl Rahners." *Wort und Wahrheit.* X (1955), 531-533.

CARMODY, J. "Karl Rahner: Theology of the Spiritual Life." *Chicago Studies.* VIII (1969), 71-86.

————, "Rahner's Spiritual Theology." *America.* CXXIII (1970), 345-347.

CARR, A. "Theology and Experience in the Thought of Karl Rahner." *Journal of Religion.* LIII (1973), 359-376.

DE LETTER, P. "The Theology of God's Self-Gift." *Theological Studies.* XXIV (1963), 402-422.

DULLES, A. "The Ignatian Experience as Reflected in the Spiritual Thought of Karl Rahner." *Philippine Studies.* XIII (1965), 471-494.

ERNST, C. "Some Themes in the Theology of Karl Rahner." *Irish Theological Quarterly.* XXXII (1965), 251-257.

GALLI, A. "Perchè Karl Rahner nega la visione beatifica in Cristo." *Divinitas.* XIII (1969), 417-456.

GEISSEI, H. "Die Interpretation der kirchlichen Lehre vom Gottmenschen bei Karl Rahner, S.J." *Kerygma und Dogma.* XIV (1968), 307-330.

HILL, W. "Uncreated Grace: A Critique of Karl Rahner." *The Thomist.* XXVII (1963), 333-356.

KENNY, J.P. "Reflections on Human Nature and the Supernatural." *Theological Studies.* XIV (1953), 280-287.

LEVI, A. "The Religious Teaching of Karl Rahner." *The Month.* XXXIV (1965), 234-245.

LINDBECK, G. "The Thought of Karl Rahner, S.J." *Christianity and Crisis.* XXV (1965), 211-215.

McCOOL, G. "The Philosophy of Human Person in Karl Rahner's Theology." *Theological Studies.* XXII (1961), 537-562.

MACQUARRIE, J. "Theologians of Our Time: Karl Rahner, S.J." *Expository Times.* LXXIV (1963), 194-197.

MASSON, R. "Rahner and Heidegger: Being, Hearing and God." *The Thomist.* XXXVII (1973), 455-488.

METZ, J.B. "Karl Rahner: Rundgang durch sein Arbeitsfeld." *Korrispondenzblatt des Canisianums, Innsbruck.* XC (1956/1957), 57-62.

——, "Karl Rahner — ein theologisches Leben." *Stimmen der Zeit.* CXCII (1974), 305-316.

MOTHERWAY, T., "Supernatural Existential." *Chicago Studies.* IV (1965), 79-103.

NEUMANN, K. "Suchen und suchend verstehen. Die Christologie Karl Rahners." *Christ in der Gegenwart.* XXVI (1974), 221-236.

NIEL, H. "The Old and the New in Theology: Rahner and Lonergan." *Cross Currents.* XVI (1966), 463-480.

O'MEARA, T. "Karl Rahner, Theologian." *Doctrine and Life.* XVII (1967), 21-37.

PEARL, T. "Dialectical Panentheism: On the Hegelian Character of Karl Rahner's Key Christological Writings." *Irish Theological Quarterly.* XLII (1975), 119-137.

QUINN, E. "Hearers of the Word: Discussion of Hörer des Wortes." *The Downside Review.* LXVIII (1950), 147-157.

RATZINGER, J. "Heil und Geschichte." *Wort und Wahrheit.* XXV (1970), 3-14.

SILOS, L. "A Note on the Notion of 'Selbstvollzug' in Karl Rahner." *Philippine Studies.* XIII (1965), 461-470.

SQUIRE, A. "Karl Rahner: A Spiritual Portent." *New Blackfriars.* XLIX (1969), 410-416.

SURLIS, P. "Rahner and Lonergan on Method in Theology." *Irish Theological Quarterly.* XXXVIII (1971), 187-201, and XXXIX (1972), 23-42.

SWEENEY, J.F. "Recent Developments in Dogmatic Theology." *Theological Studies.* XVII (1956), 368-413.

TERRETTI, G. "La filosofia della religione come antropologia in un'opera di Karl Rahner." *Rivista di filosofia neo-scolastica.* LVI (1964), 96-106.

VACEK, E. "Development within Rahner's Theology." *Irish Theological Quarterly*. XLII (1975), 36-49.

VAN ROO, W. A. "Reflections on K. Rahner's *Kirche und Sakrament*." *Gregorianum*. XLIV (1963), 465-500.

4. *Related Works*

ALLMEN, J.-J. v., *Worship: Its Theology and Practice*. Translated by H. Knight and W. F. Fleet. London, 1965.

BEVAN, E. *Symbolism and Belief*. London, 1962.

BILLOT, L. *De Verbo Incarnato*. 9th Edition. Rome, 1949.

BOROS, L. *The Moment of Truth*. Translated by G. Bainbridge. London, 1965.

BRUNNER, E. *Das Symbolische in der religiösen Erkenntnis*. Tübingen, 1914.

CIRNE-LIMA, C., *Der personale Glaube*. Innsbruck, 1959.

COOPER, J. C. *The New Mentality*. Philadelphia, 1969.

DENZINGER, H., and SCHÖNMETZER, A., eds. *Enchiridion Symbolorum, Definitionum et Declarationum de Rebus Fidei et Morum*. 32nd Edition. Barcelona, 1963.

ELIADE, M. *Images and Symbols*. Translated by P. Mairet. New York, 1961.

FAWCETT, T. *The Symbolic Language of Religion*. London, 1970.

FIRTH, R. *Symbols: Public and Private*. Ithaca, New York, 1973.

GAETSCHENBERGER, R. *Anfangsgründe einer Erkenntnistheorie*. Karlsruhe, 1920.

GILKEY, L. *Naming the Whirlwind: The Renewal of God-Language*. Indianapolis, 1969.

GRILLMEYER, A., and BACHT, H., eds. *Das Konzil von Chalkedon*. 3 Vols. Würzburg, 1954.

GUARDINI, R. *Von heiligen Zeichen*. Mainz, 1927.

GUTWENGER, E. *Bewusstsein und Wissen Christi*. Innsbruck, 1960.

KAISER, Th. *Die gottmenschliche Einigung in Christus als Problem der spekulativen Theologie seit der Scholastik*. Munich, 1968.

KELLY, J. N. D. *Early Christian Doctrines*. 2nd Edition, New York, 1960.

LANGER, S. K. *Feeling and Form*. New York, 1953.

LONERGAN, B. *Method in Theology*. New York, 1972.

MARSILI, S. *Teologia Liturgica*. Vol. II: *Mistero Pasquale del N.T.* Ad usum privatum. Rome: Pontificio Ateneo S. Anselmo, 1973.

MUSSNER, F. *Die Auferstehung Jesu*. Munich, 1969.

OLIVAN, A. *Il nuovo calendario liturgico*. Torino, 1973.

OTT, L. *Fundamentals of Catholic Dogma*. Translated by Patrick Lynch. Cork, 1954.

OTTO, R. *Das Heilige*. 6th edition. Breslau, 1921. English Translation: *The Idea of the Holy*. Translated by J. W. Harvey. London, 1972.

PANNENBERG, W. *Grundzüge der Christologie*. Gutersloh, 1964.

————. *Was ist der Mensch? Die Anthropologie der Gegenwart im Lichte der Theologie*. Göttingen, 1968.

PELIKAN, J. *The Christian Tradition*. Vol. I: *The Emergence of the Catholic Tradition (100-600)*. Chicago, 1971.

PITTENGER, N. *Christology Reconsidered*. London, 1970.

PROGOFF, I. *The Symbolic and the Real*. New York, 1963.

RICOEUR, P. *The Symbolism of Evil.* Translated by E. Buchanan. Boston, 1967.

RIEDLINGER, H. *Geschichtlichkeit und Vollendung des Wissens Christi.* Vol. XXXII of *Quaestiones Disputatae.* Freiburg, 1966.

SCHEFFCZYK, L., ed. *Grundfragen der Christologie heute.* Vol. LXXII of *Quaestiones Disputatae.* Freiburg, 1975.

SCHLESINGER, M. *Grundlagen und Geschichte des Symbols.* Berlin, 1912.

STRYNKOWSKI, J. *The Descent of Christ among the Dead.* Unpublished dissertation. Rome: Pontifical Gregorian University, 1972.

THURIAN, M. *The Eucharistic Memorial.* Translated by J. G. Davies. 2 Vols. Vol. I: *The Old Testament.* London, 1960. Vol. II: *The New Testament.* London, 1961.

ZAHRNT, H. *The Question of God.* Translated by R. A. Wilson. New York, 1969.

ALFARO, J. "Cristo Glorioso Revelador del Padre." *Gregorianum.* XXXIX (1958), 222-270.

AA. VV. *Blätter für die Philosophie.* I (1928), no. 4. Entire issue on symbolism.

DEHNE, C. "Roman Catholic Popular Devotions." *Worship.* XLIX (1975), 446-460.

GILKEY, L. "Symbols, Meaning and the Divine Presence." *Theological Studies.* XXXV (1974), 249-267.

GRILLMEYER, A. "Christologie." *Lexikon für Theologie und Kirche.* 2nd edition, 1958. Vol. II, Col. 1156-1166.

McBRIAN, J. "Incarnation and Eschatology." *Cord.* XIV (1964), 211-216.

McCool, G. "The Primacy of Intuition." *Thought.* XXXI (1962), 57-73.

POWER, D. "Symbolism in Worship: A Survey." *The Way.* XIII (1973), 310-324; XIV (1974), 57-66; XV (1975), 56-64; 137-146.

SERRADIO, E., and TURCHI, N., "Simbolo." *Enciclopedia Italiana.* Vol. XXXI, 795.

WINKLER, R. "Die Frage nach dem symbolischen Charakter der religiösen Erkenntnis." *Christentum und Wissenschaft.* 1929, 252-267.

5. Unpublished Sources

Interview with Karl Rahner, Munich, Dec. 21, 1975.
Letter of P. Pierre Jounel, Jan. 20, 1976.